AF387265

Maher Asaad Baker

The Holy Mosaic

ISBN Softcover: 978-3-384-33634-7

ISBN Hardback: 978-3-384-33635-4

ISBN E-Book: 978-3-384-33636-1

ISBN Large print: 978-3-384-33637-8

Cover image designed by Freepik

Contents

Introduction

Any conversation regarding religious matters is automatically accompanied by heated passion and people's beliefs in varying measures. These concerns stem from the social and individual worth of religious activities and attributes because these bear specific characteristics of each religious system.

Religion is another important and secret aspect of the personality of an individual and the group. It deals with the perception of the world, the system of ethical and moral values, and some of the practices that people follow. As with most topics that lie in the sphere of religion and faith, it is extremely simple for any dialogue to turn into an aggressive argument as soon as possible since people have a strictly personal and vested interest in the affairs of the soul. Therefore, these concerns are worsened by past enmity, ethical differences, and community standards. It is against these sensitivities that any dialogue has to be framed and this is why they have to be cardinal respected.

Religion is another form of complexity that is present in a classroom because people are of different beliefs and that takes time and careful observation in such a way that one does not offend any person in the class or that the teacher does not say anything that goes against the religion of any candidate, as much as he will want to do so. Tolerance in religious points refers to the acceptance of people's faiths without regard to their faith. This eschews any bias against any particular religion, to the extent that there shall be no crucial matter that shall be doused by religious bigotry. In this case effect can be constructive for example: better perception, reduced stereotypes, and better relations from such dialogues.

Syria stands in the middle of many cultures and throughout the years, has been host to Christians, Muslims, Jews, and all other forms of minorities. These are some of the few social interactions that all these communities unlike in the past and even in the present years where wars are evident have mostly manifested in terms of tolerance, sharing, and at times even worship. This is a country that has a very vibrant historical and cultural practice thus researching on religious tolerance has a worthy ground in Syria.

For instance, the Umayyad period extended from 661 to 750 CE: Syria was full of learning activities. In matters of religion, the Umayyad Caliphate allowed people to practice their choice of religion without fear hence followers of all religions exercised their freedom in worshiping. The leaders of the Islamic armies encouraged the building of gigantic religious buildings where the theme of symmetry is apparent – the Umayyad Mosque in Damascus.

References to historical cases also tend to indicate the following: dialogue is the key to understanding the dangers of intolerance. Discussion helps to comprehend situations and each other, eliminate prejudices and prejudices, and establish a conversation between representatives of different states and cultures. Such a policy of tolerance is not a mere decoration, but a tangible result of the respect for the ruling religion by the non-Muslims and the establishment of free communication with them during the Umayyad period.

The lessons from history are clear: as such it has been established that dialogue is very crucially important in the promotion of respect in the matters of religion. It enables an individual to pass an opinion that he or she has, get to know other people's opinions and possibly come to an agreement. This process of socialization is inherent in the process of building such societies which are free from violence and discrimination.

To a great extent, popular media has become the key interpreter of religion in late modernity. People from various facilities such as media stations, social media, and show businesses play a major role in how various beliefs are recorded and perceived. In this way, media plays a crucial role in educating people and fostering tolerance or serving as an instrument for strengthening prejudice and prejudices.

For example, while reporting events they regard this religion, the news coverage will mainly report events such as violence, and extremism. This can create a rather twisted view of some religions, enabling the growth of fear and prejudice, among other things. Whereas, on the contrary, the positive stories of representation of interfaith relations and religious tolerance give people a new reason to believe in something better and learn tolerance.

Media houses have a duty to provide accurate content regarding religious organizations in order to reduce the polarization of the community. This includes offering background information, not embellishing the information passed to the readers, as well as presenting different views on the given issue. Media practitioners especially journalists must ways be impartial in their presentation, giving balanced information on all the events.

This has been especially brought out by religious dialogue meetings which bring together followers of different religions. These are programs that gather leaders and subjects from various religions for the purposes of dialogue. There are real achievements in interfaith discussions and these include the signing of declarations, the creation of joint projects and recognition of the need for educational programs.

Some of the stakeholders are religious leaders and scholars, diplomats and Civil society organizations. These individuals and groups use various approaches to moderate these conversations.

Effective methods for ensuring balanced conversations include effective methods for ensuring balanced conversations include:

Establishing Ground Rules: One must always ensure that everyone attends to business with the right behavior towards the other person or even as a group.

Active Listening: Further, participants should be encouraged to listen carefully to what the other person has to say hence improving empathy.

Inclusive Representation: Appealing to all the faiths and considerations that are available out there when developing the discussions more readily leads to a well-rounded talk.

Educational Initiatives: Educational resources and programs which would help people to become religiously literate.

Interreligious respect and understanding, on the other hand, is a preserve of local communities. In practical terms, grassroots ventures can be highly effective in the work of raising tolerance within communities of different beliefs. Such activities can include the organization of one-day camps, seminars and even programs that build linkages with other religions.

For instance, mosques, churches, synagogues and temples should be premises for interfaith cooperation and discussions. These are areas whereby people of different faiths and religions come into contact, exchange ideas as well as undertake similar activities.

That is why there is nothing as powerful as civil society organizations as they are required in the achievement of the goal of harmonious existence. They make it possible for local communities to take responsibility for the future of their interfaith work, and the development of sustainable solutions to fuel religious clashes. These movements may include the use of volunteers, community elders, or youth organizations who advocate for the equality of all especially out of any discrimination.

Introducing grassroots activities, we can name interfaith camps for youth, charitable activities, and cultural events, including the ones that promote religious tolerance. These activities do not only enhance the knowledge but also the bonding and the unity of purpose of the participants involved.

It is evident that religious matters call for precautions on account of their sensitivity around the world: all these must be exercised with concern of respect and neutrality and yet be effective in their impact. The religious experience in Syria to a certain extent shows that despite differences, dialogue is possible; the result is tolerance. All media of today's epoch perform the important function of influencing the religious views of society and bear the duty of putting forward an objective scenario.' Analyzing the interfaith dialogue, one could conclude that it has acrimonious various outcomes: diplomatic levels, with the matters being discussed by religious representatives, have so far been more productive, however, it tends to stay within the frameworks of the international religious organizations, grass-root levels on the other hand, maybe less formal in terms of the outcomes achieved; however, they provide for the means of deliberating the matters of inter-religious tolerance

It is by being able to encourage open dialogue, present the whole story, and address local communities that the world will become a more open and tolerant one. The problems are daunting, yet the possible impact for the better is enormous. People of the world share one common dream that stands wrapped up in religious differences and become impatient with the only explorations that might lead to that dream's realization.

Ancient Syria

Syria in antiquity occupied the region of the eastern coast of the Mediterranean Sea, which provided it with a rather advantageous place in relation to the trading and migratory routes unifying the largest ancient states of Africa, Asia, and Europe. It was also geographically advantageously situated and had been involved in cultural and exchange of goods for thousands of years which exposed the inhabitants of the region to various cultures languages technologies and religions. Such a crossroad throws caregivers a unique and very rich Syrian identity of people who only surly developed themselves despite the up and down swinging conquerors and rulers.

The Levant of today is the ancient Syria which occupied most of the area that now belongs to Syria and parts of Lebanon. The region features considerable topographical diversity spanning four major areas: a narrow strip of territory along the Mediterranean, two huge chains of mountains along its eastern and northern borders and large tracts of interior tablelands and plains. Each part had profound differences in terms of agricultural, industrial and cultural life.

The plain is a relatively small strip of land near the Mediterranean Sea in the western portion of Syria; on the east, it is bounded by the Lebanon and Anti-Lebanon mountains. With a total length of about 193 miles, it runs from the north to the south with an increase toward the south. The north coastal region of the Levant was relatively more populated and economically active as was also more productive because of the additional supply of water and wood. The other mountain system is Lebanon and Anti-Lebanon stretching southwest-northeast and having a top elevation of 10,000 ft. These ranges enjoyed the Mediterranean rainfall for the rivers and farming in the inland valleys. Their heights also provided a measure of safety, any materials such as timber and some form of shelter that could count for something against the continental climate of the region.

In the rear of these mountains are situated the Syrian interior plains and plateaus. The northernmost plain comprises the Orontes River and the long Nahr al-'Asi (Orontes valley). The space was one of the most productive and populated areas of Ancient Syria where the Orontes river played a significant role in irrigation. Beyond these are the steppes of inner Syria, which slope steadily upward, eastwards, to the tablelands of the Syrian Desert. There is also a decline in rainfall from the sea and thus inner plains and plateaus are not suitable for the operation of the business. However, these places were still preferable for cattle ranching. The far eastern area is the Syrian Desert which is a subset of the Arabian Desert. It consists of highlands of limestone that are highly soluble land that receives an average of less than 4 inches of rainfall yearly.

Mediterranean climate is wet and cold during winter and hot and dry during summer as a result of the Mediterranean wind. The coastal parts, though have relatively high rainfall of about 40 inches per year. This is advantageous to winter-grown crops like the. Towards the East it goes gradually more and more into the interior zones and in the process becomes more and more desertlike. Fresh and portable water is limited in Syria and is obtained from melted snow from the mountains, winter rainfall and a few rivers. The Orontes is the longest of the rivers on the map and it runs through the Nahr al-'Asi agricultural plain. Meanwhile, the Euphrates runs along the borderline of the Eastern Syria. In essence, settlement and agriculture in this region for thousands of years are inextricably related to these few waterways of the region.

The position of Ancient Syria made it easy to be the link between great early-world civilizations in Africa Asia and Europe. Socially it linked the large Mediterranean Sea trading nations and the overland trade links including the silk route through Asia. It has natural harbors and geographical features that facilitate migration and barter trade exchange.

But this position also left the Syrians vulnerable to invasion by massive rival empires throughout history as well as at the same time, or concurrently.

Agricultural potential is related by its very nature to rainfall in a region as well as water availability through rivers, water tables or irrigation water. This geographical blessing and curse are revealed through and through the development of cropping sequences. Other rainfed winter crops such as wheat and barley are also widely grown in the areas of the rainy coast. Wine making was also one of the old occupations in western Syria and wine used to be exported. Fruits and vegetables and pulses required irrigation and were produced near the main water channels including the Orontes River supplying the inland Nahr al'Asi plain. At the same time, the inner plain/plateau areas of Syria were more suitable for raising of livestock, goats, sheep and some cattle. Olives destined for the production of olive oil were another major export crop, grown in regions of low rainfall. As was the case with the Phoenicians, many other ancient Syrian communities were involved in big regional trade in which they purchased food products from regions that were farther and ensured that there was enough food to support the community.

Access to water and arable land were the two criteria by which, in antiquity, the appearance of Syrian cities and rural settlements was decided. These are the coastal and inland plains, and these offered resources as exemplified by the siting of the great ancient cities of Syria. Byblos Sidon and Tyre, cities depended on Mediterranean Sea trading and agricultural land. further inland such important cities as those of Aleppo, Ebla, the Hama area, Qatna and many others developed along one of the Orontes tributaries or some other water courses. Some claim rural people singled out sites offering approximately sources of fresh water in the form of springs or strategic plains and engaged in farming grains and minimal cattle. Because of the susceptibility to floods and human attack, most of the urban had a surrounding wall. On the one hand, indigenous people living in the inner plains and plateaus are generally transhumant stock-herders with their cattle.

Ancient Syria's location facilitated extensive overland trade along two vital corridors: For instance, there was the North-South from Egypt, Syria to Anatolia – and the most well-known East-West linking China to the Mediterranean. Other famous centres that contributed to exportation included Byblos which traded famous Lebanese cedar and other resources to other nations. Land routes adopted by the caravans for the transportation of goods included the following: spices, textiles, stones and metals. Syria was also conducting intensive foreign trade relations with seaport areas within the Mediterranean; it interacted with the Aegean Sea societies and Ancient Egypt. These trade routes thus exposed the Syrians to outside technologies, cultural practices, languages and beliefs for thousands of years and at the same time exposed them to invaders.

The major world trade and migration crossroads in that part of the world led to a complex mix of people and languages in ancient Syria. The various Semitic nomadic tribes such as the Amorites and Canaanites from around the Arabian Peninsula are thought to be the first occupants. The coastal cities also had intense activities with many other Mediterranean Sea cultures, the proto-Phoenician city-states which traded with the vast Mediterranean Sea. Another early Indo-European migration to Syria was by the Hittites who established an empire in the Anatolian region and occupied many of the Syrian city-states by 1340 BC. The Semitic languages are believed to belong to the Afro-Asiatic family which, among others, boasts Arabic and Hebrew. The earliest writing system known in Syria is the cuneiform which dates to more than 3200 BC, while other Alphabetic writing systems came up around 1600 BC.

The religious beliefs before the start of the major common era involved the burning of rituals as well as sacrificial ceremonies to the Semitic, Mesopotamian and Hurrian gods. Afterlife was another early concept that was adopted merely by the cultures of ancient

Syria. All groups participated in monumental tombs, equipped with rich burial provisions and intended for the deceased to be equipped for the journey in the afterlife. For the elite, the tombs comprised either sun-dried brick chambers or chambers that had been hewn in stone, originating from nearby Ras Shamra-Ugarit or brought down to Ai from far north.

Until they coalesced into large ones, Syria had been composed of small societies that were typically a single city-state with walls. These city-states were the same Semites with a related culture but most of them quarreled to seize the fertile and the strong positions of Syrian territories. Some of the major city-states are Ebla which was one of the first kings in Syria about 2,500 and was overpowered by the Akkadian Empire, and Ugarit, a monarchical city-state that played a role in the development of the alphabetic writing. The Yamhad Kingdom was later to become the largest Hurrian and Hittite Kingdom in north Syria with its capital Halab controlling most of Syria. In the latter period, the Sea Peoples crashing and the destruction of the Late Bronze Age empires again led to the decentrally operating Phoenician period starting from the twelfth century BC where Sidon, Tyre and Byblos among others were coastal city-states that controlled wealthy seaborne trade in the Mediterranean.

In the ANE, religion can hardly be discussed without also addressing civic and personal domains intertwined together. Later millennia saw the rise of the huge monotheistic religions of Judaeo-Christian and Islamic hegemony, but the early people of Syria were animists, anthropomorphists, ancestor worshippers and polytheists. Nature is alive with inspiring spirits that in one way or another interfered in incidents concerning man, for example, rainfall or fertility. A second type of dependency was heirs; the burials as well as sacrifices were done for the guiding of the ancestors into the other world which was always regarded to have a link with the future of the living heirs. At the same time, gods were depicted and described in terms of the anthropomorphic figures associated with natural constellations or supernatural forces such as storms, death and the like.

Before 1000 BCE Syria had the gods of Mesopotamia, Egyptians, Phoenicians, and Hurrians in the pantheon of the region. Some of them are the following: Elyon – the chief god of the Levant pantheons associated with the city of Byblos and was considered equivalent to the Mesopotamian Enlil. His son Baal was a storm god accepted by the Canaanites and as far as the Old Testament is concerned, he was portrayed as a wicked character. In contrast, Anat, the ancient Semitic goddess associated with war and the creation of the god El, was depicted as Baal's sister and even friend in myth. Indeed, she was of special concern in Ugarit. Mot was another of the recurring characters and represented death and the underworld and, in turn, seasonally defeated then was resurrected from Baal in a nature myth of the rain, drought and revival tried the basic concept of a mythological deity of. Other deities who frequently feature included the sun goddess known as Shapash; Yarih who was the god of the moon; as well as Yam, the sea god. Temples of major gods using cult stelae and cult images/emblems were part of the town plan and the houses of the nobility. Kings also commonly acted as priests or prophets and commanding generals; in addition to wielding the 'theological' power, kings held material power over affairs of state, including economic and military systems.

Still, at this time of polytheism of natural deities, the Syrian religious ideas were in the course of transition to the unity of commandment and institutionalized cult. This is observed wherever one finds organization in the pantheonic Godheads such as El and in the mythologies of the natural elements imported into the human domain where justice and order are assigned and respect for old age is advocated. Thus, the first currents of 'organized religion' arose as tendencies toward urbanization and political centralization increased. The client-patron model of obedience /worship from humans indicated the dawn of the new more advanced theological concept of new faiths such as Christianity with a single supreme power in God/Jesus. Therefore, the early spiritual tradition of Syria played the role of formation of the traditions that were taken and developed by further religious movements and organizations.

The Levant was the setting for the emergence and evolution of regional cultures which were in parallel with and influenced each other for many centuries. Some of the more well-known groups included the Canaanites, Aramean and most especially the Phoenicians. It is in the region that the Canaanites penetrated in the earliest part of the third millennium BCE. Modern scholars obtain the name Canaan from the Akkadian language, where the term refers to a land occupied by a group of tribes speaking a branch of the Semitic languages. The Canaanites never ganged up together to form an empire or a common state. What was missing were nearly autonomous city-states with something like even a hazy demarcation along their edges. The Arameans were the Semitic tribal federation from the late north Arabian Peninsular BCE The clans were nomadic and inhabited in the desert of Mesopotamia and the Levant region. The Aramaic language seemed to gain a rather large following and so it transitioned into becoming a pidgin language. The Canaanite city-states would become by the first millennium BCE, wealthy traders and they would develop a culture different from their neighbors, coastal Phoenicia; such entanglement can be attributed since it can be seen to have contributed to the definition of the cultural Levantine societies of the first.

The Levant region has been occupied successively in different archaeological periods; some sites have even been estimated to be twenty thousand years old. These factors include the diversification of the geography and of the resources that where possible there, the strategic role of the region as the exchange center of the commercial roads connecting different parts of the Ancient world, the chances of forming early societies crossly to the cultures, languages and the political systems. From the late fourth millennium BC the process of urbanization becomes somewhat different.

Levantians of the ancient period displayed great advancement in social organization, technology, weaponry, arts and writing skills. They were of great influence in connecting people of different civilizations owing to enhanced networking. They were important not only for defining and developing the regional civilizations' images but also for the intensive interaction and circulation of ideas, resources and technologies. That tradition is still visible to this present day.

Canaan which was already occupied in the early 3rd millennium BCE had city-states and a culture that showed Maison Royale features, Monuments, Metallurgy and styles in pottery that were distinct from the rest Canaan had an aristocracy class. Canaanite religion availed for ancestor cult in sacrifice and temple service for city gods. Deified kings imply that there was a rather progressive polity that could accommodate the social overclass. The Egyptian hieroglyphs were further evolved into a proto-Canaanite script which is one of the earliest true forms of Alphabet by 1900 BC. Canaanites employed complex which they applied on ivory, wooden objects, metals and architecture to disseminate cosmopolitan Levantine style and décorations. He had adopted a basic economic foundation for the region, through the manufacturing of huge proportions of olive oil for export.

The Arameans were directly associated with the nomads of the Middle-Late second millennium BCE Syrian steppe, who changed their places according to the seasons and their cattle. The pastoral had basically a reciprocal exchange deal with the farmers who engaged in farming for a living. For centuries, the Arameans, who used the Semitic language, lived among the Levantines; the Aramaic dialects extended across the Fertile Crescent by 1200 BCE. This mobile existence precluded the collection of material cultural objects, however, and so Arameans are known primarily from external textual traditions and scriptural references. Last, those large Aramean monarchies united the tribes of shepherds into a massive force that proved to be capable not only of impacting and creating confusion in the old Mesopotamian kingdoms but actually becoming incorporated into them. In the course of the 10th century BCE, Aramaic was expanded as the international language in diplomacy and trade in the regions of Mesopotamia and Levant.

From among the great city harbor fortresses (Tyre, Sidon, Byblos, Arwad), there emerged the distinctive Phoenician civilization in the last part of the 3rd millennium BCE associated with trade and versatile and enterprising activities. A characteristic product was the purple-dyed textiles obtained from mollusk shells obtained from the sea. Able in the arts of engraving on glass and ivories, the Phoenician people developed the trade of iron smelting and salt-producing businesses and industries as well as fragrant oils as exportable products. It dealt in these products with other areas through their ship and at the same time, they imported raw materials, new technologies and ideas to Phoenicia. Most importantly, they passed one of the earliest and most efficient alphabets of history to further generations. Originally borrowed from the proto-Canaanites around 1200 BCE in cases of more free-flowing writing, such phonetic writing was also adopted among great civilizations such as the Hebrews, Arabic and Greeks among other great civilization.

Hence at the onset of the early Bronze Age, the Levant became situated in the overlap area of larger NE and Mediterranean cultures. This fostered contact and communication between cultures, products, arts, languages, technologies and beliefs of one local society and other societies in other parts of the world. Barter and trading missions, transporting artists, marriages, change of sides and colonies all summed up cultural exchange.

For instance, the Canaanites and Arameans before developing their own script, as did all the Semitic peoples of the region, adopted the cuneiform writing of the contemporary Mesopotamians, Akkadian cuneiform for writing of laws, treaties and simple accounting. Some of the myths also represented the process of civilization as Culture and the combination of religious areas. Asherah is another god from the Canaanite, Aramean and Phoenician religions that are proven by literature, artwork, and writing.

There were many such crossroads; the most important one being the Via Maris (Way of the Sea), the artery of communication between Egypt and Mesopotamia skirting the Mediterranean coast by 2000 BC Yet, the Phoenicians turned to the dominant seaborne traders between 1100 and 800 BCE when the

Phoenician commercial empire rose to its heights. Cautious and efficient, they established settlements along the shores and gained the ability to cross the Mediterranean Sea: all the way up to 800 BC they got as far as the Straight of Gibraltar or even beyond. In the same regard, rich commerce supplied artifacts and spices, metal and other products from the Arabian Peninsula, East Africa and Atlantic regions back to Levantine Cities. It also seems that these creative Levantine merchants used to barter tin purchased from Europe in exchange for gems and spices from near Asia besides other goods required by the powerful Hittites in Anatolia.

Already at the beginning of the third millennium, the first Canaanite cities Ebla, Byblos, and Ugarit had turned into market-places specialized in craft production. Foodstuff and other commodities provided a source of revenue for trade to support the urban centers with nobles and religious leaders. Such cities also imported raw materials from the Levant's hinterlands such as Lebanese cedar through which adjacent empires sought timber for palaces and temples. Trade led to the development of economic prosperity which is evident by the numerous burial sites where burial items included well-ornamented trays, cups, and other related utensils of gold and silver all over, fancy ornaments, and well-designed ceramics. So, by the 1900 ACE a dense Canaanite trading system evolved for both the caravans and the ships bringing metals textiles olives oils wines and timber all over the Mediterranean. This formed the basis for further achievement of the Phoenicians and was followed by more achievements.

Levantine workers produced fashionable ceramics, glass, ivories and metals as well as purple-colored textiles meant for barter as early as the early third millennium BCE. The archaeological excavation also exposed several thousands of clay tablets that told of the refined industry and business: manufacturing techniques, occupations, instruments, equipment, and trade in the Canaanite and Aramean centres of Ebla, Ugarit and many others. These furnish good knowledge as to production methods, division of labor and commercial organization in the pre-historic period. As hydraulic engineers, iron forgery and main architectural achievements they displayed high technological skills which boosted the economic gains highly. For instance, in the 12th century BC. bronze bowls from Canaan had highly advanced casting technology evidenced in equally thin walls all around and sharp ringing edges on the rim over and above exquisite artwork on the vessels. Thus, fixed capital in the form of skilled manpower became the basis for the emergence of the first wealth and development of Levantine societies.

As with the earliest urban civilizations, one of the prominent features of all the large Levantine cities was the vigorous markets. For example, Ebla was equipped with big merchant's residential areas including production rooms, storehouses as well as commercial buildings that formed part and parcel of the palace. Markets also existed for the regular barter of stock and simple goods, basic foodstuffs for pottery, baskets and clothing woven through a complex networking of specialization. Archaeological sources and writings examples prove that metals, woolen products, perfumed oil and need-based products, etc were floating in the stream of circulation among the participating agents. Also, the act of interacting in commercial places made rotation of people, and cultural swapping of the visiting civilization at the hub of commerce. Further, inns, taverns as well as banquet areas introduced other loci of communication and culture. Hence, ancient bazaars also acted as major 'media' for language, motifs, fashions, customs, and technology exchanges between societies.

While Amorite tribes were habitual nomadic or semi-nomadic lineages, Arameans had a fundamentally different structure of Canaanite society: resultant of which we have a rural peasant population residing in non-fortified agricultural settlements in contrast to the stone-walled city landscapes that had efficient administrative and military structures from 2500 BCA central political authority in many Canaanite large cities with poly-layered and various societal structures based on organizations and enclosing social class stratification. The kings of every city that did exist behaved like the cynosure with despotic authority supported by marriages to other kings' daughters and vice versa, mutual accommodation with neighboring monarchs and commensurate show of might in the form of a vast palace compound and a pyramid structure overtopping the city. Such lifestyles as living in walled towns were very different from free-range cattle grazing on the outskirts of the cities.

The political organization and the leadership of the early societies evolved from one group to the other; while the Canaanite city-states and most of the Phoenician ports were hereditary monarchial. It derived its power from the crown and sanctified it through divine charisma and a lot of show and bluster. For example, there is literature that argues that the scholarly discussion of the ritual temple prostitution's promise of sexual potency and fecundity magic to the kings' energy. All the clans and the priestly advisors were also involved in the decision-making process of the respective councils. This structure resembled Mesopotamia and Egypt pyramids. Pastoral societies were regulated by less centralized and more contentious power relations. Ebla is known to have had a succession problem toward the later part of its history as did Ugarit. Conventionally, the Tyrian kings would present their ancestry with reference to an eponymous hero or a founding father. Persistence of the traditional authority made the client kings administer the Levantine cities during the Greek control after the conquests by Alexander.

The testaments of archaeology show that social ranking and state formation started early, in large population centres of Canaan such as Ebla, Ugarit and Byblos. From the above discourses, it is apparent that complicated urban architecture had a solution to the shelter of the royalties, lords of the court, priests, artists, merchants, farmers, servants and slaves. For instance, the house of Queen Batmari in the ancient city of Mari in the 18th century BCE consumed textiles, oils, wines and sea foods which were produced in distant places and brought to Mari by caravans after a successful peace deal. The last subclass of elites were the temple priests and priestesses who were involved in owning agricultural lands together with commanding estates. An outstanding story of an aristocrat who received from King Ammurapi a piece of land and the serfs and the tax receipts from this piece of land is another Ugarit text. Therefore the classes of a Canaanite society were well defined and numbered as the early Canaanite society was of a patriarchal kind. Autocracy was wielded principally by monarchs, armed noblemen, clergy, and the businesspeople at the apex. Last of all, those defeated in battles, Phoenicians, and other murderous nations, criminals, and debtors were made slaves.

As a result, geography and culture are best used as an umbrella for understanding the ancient Syrian narrative to capture the historical orientation of the region. Because of its geographical position in this part of the world, connected to scores of other civilizations, and having a patchy and harsh terrain, the Middle East was ideal for trade and human movement and cultural intermingling. The two areas of interaction not only enabled the flow of goods and ideas but also brought into being the ethnic identities of the societies inhabiting the region. The historical richness and importance of ancient Syria are perfectly depicted in the variety of societies languages, and religions that inhabited the region.

Knowledge of such topographical and social characteristics, associated with historical events of human development, and early settlements that happened in this area, is essential to realize how these experiences influence the present. Studying ancient Syria is a useful cognition about how cultural exchange, economic processes, and social relations influence the vectors of historical development. Therefore, the lessons learned from them are still a very strong message that applies to the world that is interconnected as it is today.

Judaism's Emergence

In fact, Jews have lived in Syria probably as long as anyone can remember; documents confirming Jewish presence in Syria have been traced from the fourth century BCE. In the next centuries, Syria was home to significant numbers of Jewish people; Jews lived in all spheres of Syrian life within the sphere of economic and cultural activity.

It probably originated during the time of the rule of the Romans over Syria and the evacuation of the Hebrews to this place. With the broadening of trade connections through the Middle Eastern region new dwelling places were found for Jew traders through the trading centres of Syris and the place which is known today as Antioch.

Such social relationships affected the transfer of people such as when after the conquests made by Tiglath-Pileser III people from Judah were transported around the region and probably during the last part of the eighth century. The change in the social situation under different reigns contributed to the further Jewish assimilation in Syria in the next centuries.

There were local Jewish living quarters in some Syrian cities, such as Dura-Europos. They involved themselves in the local commerce as weavers, merchants as well as usurers. The major way of people remaining connected was through religion and education with synagogues and schools as the sources of connectedness. Amongst these traits, it was possible to single out the Greek-speaking ability of the Syrian Jews, and also the peculiarities of the Syrian Jewish food that can be described as the combination of Middle Eastern and Jewish dishes.

Besides the economic interaction, Syrian Jews also socially assimilated the society by writing in Aramaic. They told legends of King Solomon commanding demons to build the cities – a story of Jewish history to the region.

Judaeo-Christians were inhabitants of Syria and among them few Jewish historical personalities were mentioned including the historian Titus Flavius Josephus. The events of the First Jewish Revolt described by Josephus contain an idea of the relations between the Jews and Romans. Other personalities that were also named included Marcus Julius Agrippa and King Monobazos II who donated to the construction of the Jerusalem Temple.

To the Maccabean revolt as an uprising against religious persecution and Jewish civil wars in choosing their camp, one can trace episodes of cooperation or conflict with Hellenistic rulers in 167-160 BCE. They further cemented the pre-existing diaspora networks that were in existence between Syria and Judea.

Due to the close contact between the two nations, there were many interactions whereby Aramaic borrowed many Hebrew words and phrases as was seen among the people through marriage. The Jews also borrowed pagan practices that called the dead blessed, and festivals that were held during spring equinox. They also brought in customs in the opposite direction for instance how the Syrians used to practice some of the customs associated with Jews.

The conventional script persisted though when empires were being conquered by new ones and Jews were experiencing the circumstances of the conquerors. That is why their scriptures were translated into Greek in mid third century BC for more circulation. In the diverse world of the twenty-first century, this is an example of how the Syrian people combine the friendliness of the shared culture while still preserving the tenet of the belief in one God.

When Alexander the Great fought his battles in the 4th century BCE, Greek society displaced the Middle East – and the Syrian Jews. Such societies got an outright revolution when Greek became the common and trade language. Hellenistic ideas were felt in Jewish education and philosophy among the Jewish elites. It's reflected in the works by a Judean scholar named Philo who tried to harmonize Judaism with Classical culture.

Diaspora groups were hard in the way of having to assimilate into the cultures that prevailed while at the same time being able to remain religiously distinct. The vast majority of Jews in Syria engage Hellenism in selective manners as a cultural package – they continue with their normal local routine while mingling with other groups in a common arena. Among the most frequent means of their adaptation were translations of the

Scriptural texts to Greek and beautification by certain forms of art of Hellenistic origin but Jewish content.

However, the severe oppression by the Greek king Antiochus IV led to a Jewish Syrian uprising known as Maccabees in 167 BCE. Therefore, both the processes of adaptation and resistance were observed in Jews' behavior in different stages, which ruled out assimilation even after centuries of interaction.

This is why during the Seleucid period when the assimilation of the Jews in Syria took place, the cosmopolitan city of Antioch was especially suitable for that purpose. According to the sources from the 1st century CE, 7312 Jews were living in the territories of Antioch. Josephus mentioned some rights granted to the Jewish residents of the city. Other changes in other areas of the communal context were scholarly discourse meeting places. And it is also important to know that since the first centuries of AD Antioch was one of the centers of the development of the Christian church – which tells about the city as one of those places where intercultural and interconfessional discourse was conducted.

When Rome was setting out to firmly ensconce itself in the Middle East in 64 BCE, Syria was transformed into a province. During the early part of the Roman empire, the laws protected Jewish people's rights to pray and assemble. Some privileges were offered to Jews from Judea and they migrated to the country. However, in other years, when other emperors ruled, they instilled high taxes which caused rebellions. It came to a head during the Kittos war in 115-117 CE which compelled the emperor Hadrian to try to ban some of the core Jewish rites – with ramifications for the Jews of Syria.

One could argue that during the Roman period the Jewish identification with Hellenistic culture, and legal structures attributable to the city model, began. In general, the Jews of the Levant were bilingual because, alongside Hebrew and Aramaic, Greek was widespread. The level of integration is most obvious if one examines some examples, like Severus Sebokht, a Syrian Jew of the 6th century CE, who was an active astronomer and bishop at the same time.

During the medieval age especially the Islamic conquest, people came to know Syria as a center of Jewish studies and home of venerable scholars and jurists who contributed towards the development of Judaic law and reason and also the other physical aspects of Jewish mysticism. Some of the luminaries emerging from the Syrian Jewish community include:

Rabbi Abraham ben David of Posquières and other scholars began to come to the fore during this period.

Abraham ben David (1125–1198), known also as Ravad III or the Raavad, was one of the outstanding personalities of medieval Jewish philosophy and one of the most prominent Talmud scholars. Abraham ben David was born in Posquières, France of Jewish Syrian Tripolitanian parentage and has some exegetically interesting remarks in the book, Mishneh Torah by Moses Maimonides.

In his explanations based on Maimonides' legal works, AVI provided negative critiques of the way Maimonides proceeded and the conclusions he drew. In more detail, he challenged Maimonides on the latter's way of not indicating the sources upon which legal conclusions are based or offering them as facts. This criticism set the direction of the halachic literature because prior to this people had become more cautious in the references they made to previous authorities. The conflict between Abraham ben David and Maimonides also threw light on the controversies about one of the key issues: how the practical Talmudic law should be interpreted and implemented. Thus Abraham ben David, while the historicizing of the natural law and fixing of a set of legal positions that could support a new idealism outside of natural law is innovative, is innovative also in the sense of developing more rationalist methodologies for the creation of the Halachic legal literature which defines Jewish legal writing today.

In addition to his legal compositions, Abraham ben David authored several philosophical works of which Sefer ha-hanhagot is the most significant. This work set the foundations of a new Jewish philosophical concept that focused on the Medieval Jewish interpretations of Midrash in contrast to the Hellenism that most Jewish Medieval philosophers embraced. Hence, in his search for pure philosophic principles in Jewish source material alone, Abraham ben David also paved the way for subsequent Jewish philosophy.

The sources of Abraham ben David's inventive philosophical works were negative to his Syrian origin. Provencal Jews under the domination of the Christians constituted the leadership in the community headed by the Rabad yet they faced challenges. The position that the Jews occupied in Muslim territories was marginally safer relative to the Christian world, and this allowed Jewish philosophical reflection to continue relatively unabated. Hence, family ties with Syria may well have endowed the Rabad with the tradition of extra-biblical free philosophical reasoning derived from these older Jewish communities of the Middle East.

Jewish mysticism later on was continued through Chaim Vital (1543–1620). Vital was born in Jerusalem as his father managed to escape the wave of expulsion of Spanish and Portuguese Jews from their homeland to Syria. Vital's mother descended from the Nahmani wealthy family from Aleppo.

Vital rose to the rank of the main disciple of the Kabbalist mystical rabbi, Isaac Luria, who devoted himself to recording his teacher's concepts and lectures. Luria's ideas were systematized by Vital to explain the themes of the Lurianic cabal, Ksabbalistis, which played a very important role in the development of Jewish philosophy and rituals.

Vital published several Kabbalistic works as follows: Sha'ar HaKavvanot which is a work that expounds on kavvanot which are the intentions that concern prayer and other religious practices. Another work is called Sha'ar HaGilgulim or the Gate of Reincarnations which contains Luria's ideas on reincarnations and the transmigration of souls. His sons issued his many-volume opus

Etz Chaim (Tree of Life) which expounds the theosophy of Lurianic Kabbala.

In addition to giving sermons based on Kabbalistic concepts, Vital also recommended the performance of the commandments. His austerities have thus been stereotyped by later Kabbalists. Therefore, Vital disseminated the Lurianic Kabbalist instructions in the Mediterranean Jewish communities in order to convey these obscure doctrines to the people and entrench the Kabbalistic tradition in contemporary Judaism. Because the works reproduced by Vital turned into reading for a long period, it is possible to consider Vital as one of the greatest Kabbalists in history.

Syrian Jewish communities continued to achieve scholarly renown into the modern era through religious philosophers and community leaders who made lasting contributions to Jewish thought in the 19th and 20th centuries, Syrian Jews were able to establish themselves as scholars even in the modern period with present-day religious philosophers and community leaders who have provided lasting enlightenment to Jewish sages of the 19th and 20th century.

Rabbi Yaakov Chaim Sofer: A Sofer from Baghdad who lived in the years 1870-1939, Sofer wrote more than thirty philosophical books that included amongst them Kaf Hachaim which attempts to expound on legal matters of the Jewish people. Most of the mystical letters of reference and the many allusions to Mediterranean Jewish culture pointed out Sofer's Syrian origin. Sofer arrived in Israel in 1924 when most of the Jews in Iraq had had to flee due to growing intolerance and prejudice against them.

Rabbi Ezra Attia – He was born in the year 1885 in Aleppo, Syria and the Sephardic sages who were the members of the Porat Yosef Yeshiva in Jerusalem ordained him before he returned back to Syria. His life was devoted to Jewish education and he started the Aleppo Ateret Zvi and Ateret Yosef yeshivot in 1925 and produced thousands of rabbis. The speeches of Attia and the scholarly essays as well in Or Zaruah inspired the Syrian Jewry. His sensibilities contributed to the process of raising Aleppo to the level of a major center of mid-twentieth-century Sephardic scholarship.

Murad Beh Farag – Scholar, banker and Jewish leader in the early twentieth century in Aleppo, he died in 1956 having reconstituted the Jewish community council of Aleppo in

1918 after the council had been secret for centuries. Farag several historical works about the medieval Jewish communities of Europe, and founded and edited the Judeo-Spanish journal La Luz to promote the cultural heritage of the Jewish community of Aleppo. Nonetheless, Farag's predominantly Jewish library is still regarded as an invaluable source for research in Israel's National Library.

They are among the recent luminaries of the scholars who wrote for Syrian Jewish centres up to the modern period. Educational and scholarly levels developed in Syria through the centuries influenced the further evolution of Jewish philosophies to the maximum.

On the whole, Syrian Jews sustained a lively Jewish existence, and they had organically developed arguably all Jewish traditions, such as yeshivas, kehillas or community councils. These entities forged communal cohesion by facilitating sophisticated Torah scholarship, these entities built up shared communal identity by supporting advanced instruction in Torah.

Since the Middle Ages the communities of Syrian Jews were involved in the networks of yeshivot, the institutions for the subsequent study of the Talmud and the Torah law. As in other Syrian Jewish settlements, schools thrived in the Syrian-Jewish communities as these communities took over the role of scholarly Babylon from the Baghdadi yeshiva.

Hence, Syrian cities like the city of Aleppo were encircled with other large yeshiva such as Midrash Knesset Israel a yeshiva that was established in the year 1865, and the Yeshivat

Or Torah which was founded in 1920. That is, by the middle of the twentieth century, despite the greater volume of other Jewish communities, nine large yeshivot could be distinguished in Aleppo. Jewish students appeared to study in Syria from all over the world to acquire the best rabbinic education from erudite scholars who have a vast understanding of the theoretical and practical dimensions of Talmudic laws of business.

Besides Aleppo, the Jewish community of Damascus also created the Beit Zilkha yeshiva. Syrian Jewish yeshivot, therefore, facilitated the continued practice of the Babylonian-originated-Sephardic way of studying the Talmud by correlating it with laws' enforcement. It was this dialectic scholarly tradition that defined Jewish law for two thousand years after the Babylonian academies. Thus, it is possible to draw a line from Syrian yeshivot to the origins of Jewish legal tradition.

In parallel to educational activity, the Jewish communal councils of Syria invested a lot of money in supporting the study of the Torah. These were the councils of elders and rabbis who formerly did all the governing in the area as far as the Syrian cities were concerned. For example, the Jewish council in Aleppo was involved in financing local religious schools, supervising the delivery of kosher meat and regulating contacts with the municipality.

This autonomy is witnessed by the fact that bearing in mind the minority status of the Jews, the Ottoman and later the French Mandatory authorities allowed a significant level of self-organization. The local councils, on their part, the funds raised through taxes, and religious education were the primary concern of the community. Therefore, even the poor Jewish children had some degree of primary religious education in Syria and towns proclaimed having almost 100 percent Jewish literacy.

Money also arrived in the reverse direction as many of the most prosperous merchanting families of the community councils were investing their funds again to support religious establishments. This stability whereby successful people in the society extended their support to the financial net of the commune made Syria a producer of Jewish scholarship. These councils persist today wherever the Syrian Jewish expatriate settlement has occurred over the world as organizations that reflect concerns of Jewish life in Aleppo, Damascus and other cities of the Levant in the 19th and 20th centuries.

The learning activity of the Jewish community in Syria was thereby renewed and sustained by the effects of active and initiative spiritual leaders. These individuals advanced the state of Talmudic discourse and responded to the challenges confronting their communities. These people contributed to the improvement of the Talmudic discussion and responded to the difficulties encountered in society.

The previous scores also positioned the Chief Rabbis not only as massive law gurus but at times other real power apparatus coming from holding the post of the Rosh Av Beit Din, the head of Rabbinical courts.

Although he practiced as a Rabbi from 1756, Rabbi Isaac Lumbroso was the official Chief Rabbi of Aleppo in the 18th century.

Rabbi Salim Zafrani was the Hakham Bash(i) or the chief rabbi of Damascus in the 1800 century and left behind him numerous philosophical and legal works and responsa.

Rabbi Chaim Nahum was officially recognized as the Chief Rabbi of Aleppo in 1909 where he was described as a Talmudic and kabbalistic scholar par excellence. Traveling around Europe and Palestine, Nahum, of course, fundraised to support the religious institutions of Aleppo and victims of other Jewish disasters. Thus it has been stated that he writes often and his works remain contemporary to the modern generation.

In addition to the chief rabbis, rabbinic judges also sat to attend religious courts that dealt with issues relating to Jewish law. In the early nineteenth century, the Hakham Bashi of Safed was Rabbi Yaakov Antebi of the Safed Beit Din court; one of his prominent works was Mekor Baruch's legal work.

Lacking a polis and a political leader, the Jewish people had to rely on rhetorically persuasive rabbis. Passionate personalities such as Rabbi Moshe Malka, who after becoming the leader of the Damascus Jewish community in the first half of the nineteenth century, used speeches and fund-raising trips for the Eretz Yisrael Jews.

Chief Rabbi of Aleppo Chaim Nahum alongside merchant and later finance minister Murad Farahat was promoting Jewish modernization and integration into French rule in the 1920s over the opposition of the majority of the Jewish population, who did not support their attempts to introduce education reforms. Together they are considered as a model of the scholar-lay leader collaboration that sustained Jewish society in Syria.

Not only was there a Syrian influence, but those who were influenced by the rabbis themselves went on to become influential in other areas. For instance, in the nineteenth century, there was a man known as Rabbi Yaaqov Kuli from Damascus who devoted his efforts to the renewal of the Jewish community life in Iraq which in the course of that period became almost nonexistent. Likewise, Rabbi Ovadiah Yosef, born in Baghdad, learning under Syrian scholars, rose to become the leading Sephardic halakhic authority of the twentieth century, and formerly the chief rabbi of Israel.

Therefore, the resilience of the community must have been due to the visions of the rabbis and other leaders who sustained the tradition even if there was pressure and hostility all around them. Most of them have left great legacies which are exemplary to generations of followers up to the present times.

But Syrian Jewish societies engaged in educating rebels in secular and academic professions, as well as the religious educational institutions of the yeshivot.

Among them is the philosopher Sadiq al-Azm, who was born in Damascus in 1934 and once met the existentialist philosopher Jean-Paul Sartre in Paris to later become a teacher at the American University of Beirut. Such works as those that decried such aspects of Arab culture and politics presented him as one of the bravest modern Arab writers.

Geometric Michael Atiyah –Michael Atiyah was born, in 1929 in Alexandria and grew up in Cairo as the son of a senior partner of a large mercantile business of Syrian Jewish origin The Oxford-educated mathematician was one of the most celebrated mathematicians, of the twentieth century, internationally renowned for his work in geometry and topology. The man then proceeded to head Oxford's famous faculty of mathematics.

Prof Richar Arnowitt – Jew born in 1928 in Jerusalem of parents from Aleppo; He held the position of Professor of Physics at Texas A&M University. He is endowed with the recognition of having made the Arnowitt–Deser–Misner formalism through which geometrodynamics of spacetime is branded as crucial in Einstein's general relativity theory.

Great personalities of that period have shown that, apart from religious bigotry, the society of the period enjoyed the intellectual freedom that was seen during the previous Turkish and French occupation. This promoted interaction and coalescence with or beyond the transnational Jewish commonwealths wherein Jewish academics were engrossed.

Of course, the Middle East has always had its share of religious tolerance but it is largely true the region was somewhat more pluralistic in the past and that meant that you had real interaction between Christians, Jews and Muslims and it was not a façade. Hence, the overlapping of different Jewish communities' limits made it possible to receive recognition in non-Sephardic Jewry, even in the Muslim scholarship realm.

For example, Isaac Armillas was an 18th-century Jewish scholar who was given his position as the secretary to the Ottoman governor of Damascus as the official scribe and writing instructor of the Hebrew language. He rose to be known throughout the region as the best when it came to writing in languages, astronomy, medicine and geography among Islamic and Jewish scholars and writers.

Likewise, in the early twentieth century, there was Rabbi Nissim Bechar, an Algerian who migrated and settled in Lebanon; so much was this Rabbi accepted as a scholar of Quran and Arabic that both Sunni and Shia scholars asked him questions on Islamic law and jurisprudence known as Shari'ah and had their students study under him.

The fact that such religious pincher points were constituting positively mediating scholarly networks evidenced that something was wrong with the perception of isolated and alienated minorities. What was considered to be a cultural advantage has proved more than handy in maintaining the Jewish cultural experience in Syria to become the crucible of the creative intellectual Syrian Jewish generations who rise above parochialisms.

Those changes with which the Syrian rabbis introduced into legal interpretation and practice were unprecedented and, indeed, put an indelible imprint on the subsequent course of evolution in mainstream Ashkenasic Jewish legal tradition. Many of the responsa do cite Syrian decisions and codifiers. golah (exile). It is important to note that the given specific, technical, and systematic approach to defining characterization reflects not only the general Syrian and Sephardic trends; however it is still widely implemented in them.

Actually, following the early Syrian commentators, Rabbi Joseph Caro's most potent legal code that determines Jewish practice nowadays – Shulchan Aruch – includes the rulings. This kind of deference is visible also in later authors including 18th-century Rabbi Chaim Benveniste whose well-known commentary on Caro's work relies extensively on Syrian sources.

Likewise, huge volumes of unabridged letters that pose real-time legal concerns, written to influential Syrian rabbis, have turned into liturgical documents as a tribute to those rabbis.

Specific notable legal contributions with enduring repercussions today include, some of the particular distinctive legal contributions that have continued to have significant impacts even in the present:

A legal opinion given by the Chief Rabbi of Damascus Saul Abadie in 1755 to cope with some problems of personal status and Jewish blood due to miscegenation under the Ottomans. What is worth emphasizing is the fact that more than two centuries after his work he is providing guidelines still being in practice.

This is provided by the conditions fit the Halachic exemption that Rabbi Chaim Nahum issued in 1920 permitting the augmentation of the supply of foodstuffs to the increasing Jewish population in Syria through the shuttling that made it possible to presume that the products are kosher without supervision by local rabbis at the manufacturing origin. These standards set the criteria for kosher certification of CPC products to the present time.

Symptomatic of 20th-century antecedents to the changes that the pressures and population movements of the Middle Ages brought about for the Syrian Jewish community: Rabbi Ezra Zion Sassoon's leniencies regarding converts, doubtful marriages and mamzerim. It retained the possibilities of continuing family lineages since these adapted precedents accompanied the Jewish people when they moved around the world.

As the methods for the transport and conveyance of people and messages improved the authority of the Syrian rabbis as legal interpreters of Jewish law remained intact since even when a decision was made geographically far away from the person it could easily reach him. Rabbinic scholars of today are thereby still receiving and adding to the tapestries of deliberative processes carried out in the synagogues, yeshivot, and homes of Aleppo, Damascus, and Qamishli.

Jewish contacts with other Syrian religious groups defined a number of rather friendly interactions, which affected occasional positive attitudes towards the Jewish culture. While Jews disagreed over some occurrences, they benefited from years of accommodation and absorption.

The other aspect was that the ecclesiastical leaders and rabbis demonstrated quite a lot of similarities in the social norms they held regardless of the difference in religion. A friend of the clear Islamic scholar, Ibn Rushd (Averroes), was the 12th-century philosopher Maimonides. Both were expelled by fundamentalists in their respective religions because such people regarded philosophy as a threat because of its heirs. They are to show that the heads of organizations endure social occurrences while being segregated as requested by religious leaders.

Likewise in the early nineteenth century, the chief rabbi of Beirut Isaac Beer got a discharge from the bishop of Damascus for the Jewish colony in questions relating to interference with Eastern Orthodox Christians. Beer then advanced on the positive relationship with the church leader and then the legal argument based on similar beliefs against the disclosure of sins to the public.

It, therefore, becomes quite apparent that Jews had always been present in Syria right from the very earliest stages of the civilization of Syria in the Biblical period right up to the Hellenistic and Roman periods. Jewish figures and incidents throughout the Syrian dispersion influenced the Jewish communal and scriptural heritage across the time. With intensive trade connections to the Greeks and Romans and living in cities such as Antioch, a rich syncretism of Jewish and Hellenistic ideas was promoted. The roles of the Jewish scholars as well as leaders, and the growing communities they fostered, all played major roles in the chi Jewish life and knowledge, equally, it also opens a page in Jewish history, showing how Syria has been involved, relating to Jewish history as a whole, and telling the story of Jewish capacity and intelligence, which is evident through the numerous centuries.

Christianity's Ascendancy

Christianity developed over the course of the first century CE, from being a movement within Judaism that consisted of a number of doctrines, the ministry of Jesus Christ, and the crucifixion and subsequent resurrection of Jesus. This Jewish sect would in the space of the next three hundred years extend its dominance over the Roman empire and plant the foundations of one of the greatest religious movements of all recorded history. Thus, Christianity is tied up inextricably with Middle Eastern history in the first centuries since this is where Jesus was born and where the Church evangelized most of the time. Yet there are the crucial aspects that have to be blamed on the actions of the Roman province of Syria namely the early Christian church's dynamism with which it grew.

When Syria was occupied by the Romans in the first century it was a very cosmopolitan nation as it lies on the crossroads of many trade routes. Such an environment avails the apostle Paul and other missionaries to reach from one place to another and propagate the Lord to Jews and Gentiles. Indeed, among the first and, definitely, the most essential church formations that emerged in Syrian cities, for example, Damascus and Antioch. The church of Antioch and the patriarchs that it developed produced quite a number of doctrines formulated and propagated early in Christian theology. Syrian territory continued being conducive to new theological development of Christianity after the church organizational structure was legal in the fourth century and for bishops' authority. Thus when analysing the function of early Syrian Christianity it is possible to work out the cord that formed this religion and the people that endowed it with the morphology that it would assume throughout the historical process to bring a change to the world.

At first century CE Syria was situated in a very advantageous position as a bridge between the Eastern and the Western parts of the Roman Empire. It covered a wide geographical spread of the area in the Mediterranean. Antioch and Damascus the major cities of Syria were located along the major axis that ran from Mesopotamia in the east to Asia Minor, Greece and Italy. It also had coastal ports by which it could be accessed by sea over the Mediterranean. Due to this favorable geographical position Syrian cities became the large trading centres and the intersection of many civilizations.

Syria also had large Greek, Roman and Jewish communities during the Seleucid as well as the subsequent Roman era. The region was under the impact of the ancient Near Eastern, Greek and Roman civilizations for several centuries either by contact, conquests and settlers. This led to such features as the languages, manners, structures, and even the religious structures that are regarded as the "Greco-Roman" or the "Hellenistic" culture. Syrian society was ethnically, culturally, and religiously diverse and increasingly urbanized in large metropolitan areas.

This melting pot environment I have substantiated was pivotal in the birth of Christianity as well as the transformation of the Jewish sect into a world religion. The multicultural features of Roman Syria were beneficial to the early Christians in yet another way as compared to the other Christians of Judea in that these Christians could effectively mix and maneuver more easily in this new world. They saw other preexisting cultures that could easily be evangelized and assimilated into Christianity as the Jew's religion, which they already had a monotheistic idea of God. At the same time, Greco-Roman philosophical tendencies determined the process of the new faith's theological encoding during time.

Among the early evangelists of Christianity, the Apostle Paul stands out having been indeed an evangelist who seemed to have never ventured far from Syria and Asia Minor which is present-day Turkey. Born as Saul, a Pharisee, from Tarsus, Paul was a staunch persecutor of the new Christians, before he had his famous vision on the Damascus Road of Jesus. This entirely revised Paul's life and rather than concentrating towards diminishing the subject matter of Christianity, he focused on preaching it.

It is crucial to note that Paul was a Jew living in the diaspora, who was familiar with Greek thought, which made him capable of delivering the message of Jewish Christianity to Gentiles of the late Roman empire. With no let up, he started evangelizing in Damascus where he served God for three years until he was compelled out of the city by threats from the Jews. It was in the following three decades that he traveled around Syria and Anatolia to form Christian churches by preaching, producing miracles and writing letters.

The letters that Paul penned down were to the churches that he founded and in those, he included essentials of Christianity and likewise theology's answer to issues relevant to the fellowship. As to the views such as justification by faith in Christ, the death and the resurrection of the believers with Christ in the baptism, and the indwelling of the Holy Spirit, Paul is mainly responsible for these. Later Church Councils and theologians would refine vocabulary for these notions but Paul's epistles would offer the initial articulation of doctrine for both Jew and Gentile. This author affected early New Testament Christian thinking more than any other author in the New Testament.

The first Christian Church outside Judea started in Damascus several years after the death of Jesus Christ at around 30 CE In the New Testaments in the book of Acts of the

Apostles reveals that after Jesus was crucified, the disciples got scared for their lives to preach again, but the gathered themselves and went to preach in Jerusalem again. Acts notice that some of the Cypriot and Cyrenian Jews who became Christians wished to conduct a mission in Damascus. As much as their activities are not elaborated, the text suggests that they performed well enough to get the attention of the Jews from Damascus to 'punish' the new Christians and force them to flee the city.

Some years later the dramatic conversion of 'Paul' and the event that occurred on the road to Damascus can be considered a major shift. That is why Paul did not attempt to extinguish the newly formed movement; on the contrary, he joined it and immediately began at once to preach in the synagogues that Jesus was the Son of God. This evangelism put so much pressure on Damascus that within three years Paul decided to move to Jerusalem and then to his homeland – Tarsus of Cilicia. But there has been an unbroken line of an old church in Damascus that asserts its apostolic succession from the first Jewish-born church.

Antioch was the first place that replaced Judea as the place of organization of Christianity and in most if not all aspects became the mother church to Jerusalem. By roughly 43, however, ambassadors from Jerusalem established a far more formal council that convened in Antioch. The multi-cultural situation was convenient to collect many Gentile disciples and to smooth the ethical conflict that occurred in the Judaic church between Hebrews and Greeks. Consequently, the church at Antioch grew much faster and within ten years of its beginning, it had the strength and authority to dispatch Paul with Barnabas on a mission touring Asia Minor. By the middle of the first century, it had developed more or less into a kind of center for Christianity and its missions.

In the following centuries Antioch continued to assert the power of the five major Christian sees alongside Rome, Constantinople, Alexandria and Jerusalem. The most effective person leading the religious discourse of the time was Ignatius, the bishop of the well-known Antioch church and around 100 CE, he provided thoughts on church hierarchy, priesthood and the sacraments. On the other hand, the Didache, one of the oldest forms of the summing up of the instruction that was to be a model of the behavior of the Christians, was written in Syria at this time. Such developments serve as evidence of the fact that Syria was the land of origin of the institutions and practices that were to make

Christianity after it emerged from Judaism, an organized religion.

It was the Jewish and Greek and Near Eastern way of life that contributed to the theological formation of Christianity it also played its part in filling up the lacunae that the founder of Christianity failed to do. But what Rabbinic Judaism was able to offer was ethical monotheism drawn from divine communication and the Mosaic legalism. It is noted that Aristotelianism and neo-Platonism transposed philosophic notions such as logos, Sophia, pneuma, arete and psyche/psychic and others. Mystery cults connected to the dying-rising savior gods of the ancient Near East provided a paradigm for the crucifixion narratives in the New Testament and the Eucharist. The early Syriac Christians thus adopted from the culture that they found around them absorbing and allocating the new product in accordance with the new religion that they were now establishing.

It seems that the Graeco-Roman language and philosophy played an especially important role in the first centuries of the development of Christian teaching. At the time of Jesus, Koine Greek had evolved into the official language of the Gentiles in Syria. That is why both the Septuagint Old Testament and the Greek New Testament also affected the way the Hebrew biblical text was viewed in the light of Hellenistic culture. It is worth mentioning that when Church Fathers of Syrian origin had to express the actual reality of the Triune Godhead and the personhood of Christ in terms of philosopheme, they adopted Greek terms like ousia and hypostasis. Belief was often explained in terms of Greek terminology and categorization, hence, whenever the different sets of thoughts engaged in a battle of words over a particular word being vague, or the meaning of a word having been misunderstood, it turned into heated arguments. However, the adoption of Greek philosophy and style did continue the growth of Christian doctrine by thus presenting it in terms comprehended by Gentiles.

It was in the course of this period that theologians from Syria contributed important ideas on the vital theological concerns that were taken during the Nicene period. Sometimes Christology of Beryllus of Bostra who opposed the view that Jesus was not present before his incarnation was sharply answered and corrected by another Syrian Bishop Eusebius of Caesarea who supported the theory of divinity of Christ. Eustathius of Antioch complained, for instance, against a group like Origenists for their excessive integration of pagan philosophy into theology.

While Arius stirred up a great storm in the church through this statement: 'He was not always' or 'There was a time when he was not,' Eustathius like other Syrian bishops, went to the council of Nicaea in which Arianism was condemned and the doctrine of the Trinity was upheld. In any case, the theological dialogue initiated by Syrians did not remain barren of conflict and also contributed to the early development of Christianity's critical self-reflection and its vocabulary for thinking about the very heart of the matter: the mystery of the Incarnation of God in Jesus Christ.

Luther is accompanied by his apostle Paul of Tarsus, and, apart from those two, many other Syrian saints and churchmen are of great historical value. Peter, designated as chief apostle, chosen by Jesus to lead the twelve, is also rather emphasized in the Acts as taking a strong part in the founding of the church at Antioch before transferring his episcopal see to Rome. He had put one of the first Antiochene bishops Evodius by 42 CE with the help of Barnabas another assistant of Paul and a Levantine Jew He also made measures by building the city of Antioch into the pillar of gentile Christianity.

Bishops that succeeded the first ones such as Ignatius and Theophilus continued with the formulation of Antioch's Christian leadership by writing on the church's structure and governance as well as engaging in war with other groups deemed to be heretical. At the same time, Ephrem the Syrian wrote great hymns and homilies, moreover, he can be considered as the most vital theologian of the early Syrian theological school according to the tendencies of the Oriental Orthodoxy. It would be important to mention other Syrian theologians who seem to be engaged in the early debates; Diodore, and Theodore who were recommended by Antioch for the episcopacy though other provinces disagreed.

Thus, for decades, centuries and millennia there emerged a split in the theological and linguistic terms that the Eastern Greek Church and the Western Latin Church used after the Council of Chalcedon 451 CE which stated that Jesus was fully man as well as fully God. Such tensions were pointed at their extreme in the Acacian Schism of 484 AD in which Roman Catholicism and the Eastern Orthodoxy have been alienated for 35 years before the Great Schism occurred six centuries later. It was in Syria itself that these intense Christological disputes which were the cause of this division were first fanned: it was the place of the first gentile converts. Indeed, those thoughts that were theological Syrian or those thoughts that were circling around the patriarchs and teachers of Antioch and in relation to early Christianity as well had their part represented into the framing of early Christianity which added several succeeding ages to the church history of the world.

Antioch is one the oldest cities in the world and was established in 300 BCE by Seleucus I Nicator. Antioch on the Orontes was a metropolitan in the western part of present-day Turkey at the meeting point of Asia Minor and the Mediterranean coastal strip adjacent to Syria. In the first centuries of Christianity, the Antiochian city turned into the third most significant city of the Roman empire with a population of around 400,000 – 500,000. It also flourished in business because of its location mainly in marketing regions; and was multiculturally inhabited by the Greeks, Romans, Jews and Persians.

And it was to this overcrowded and culturally diverse city that one of the largest concentrations of Christians beyond Judea started to emerge in the years subsequent to the crucifixion of Jesus Christ. The history of the early Mission is recorded in the Acts of the Apostles some of the earliest missionary work took place in Antioch after the stoning of Stephen in Jerusalem which led to other Christians being forced out of Judea. However, the name 'Christians' was first used for the disciples in Antioch emphasizing the importance of the city for the new religion. This newly born start-up of Christianity advanced much with the account of Barnabas and Paul, two itinerate preachers who came to Antioch for nearly a full year and turned the place into a major church touring zone. From Antioch, there and then with the others, Paul's missionary journeys would start to spread the gospel to the Jews and Gentiles in other places.

According to the sources, the first bishop to lead the church in Antioch at the start of the 2nd century AD was Evodius. Among some of the scholars who are associated with Antioch include Ignatius of Antioch who wrote substantial letters on theological matters while he was on his way to Rome to be martyred. Another saint – John Chrysostom was to appear several centuries later, as one of the outstanding leaders of the early church who rose to the rank of an Archbishop of Constantinople; He left behind a huge, influential mark on Eastern Orthodoxy and other strands of early Christianity. It took over the next few centuries for Antioch to distinguish itself not only as the location of an important Christian church but as the birthplace that gave central theology and some of the chief apostolic personalities that the Christian church needed to bring the message of Christ to the Roman Empire.

From the second and third centuries, Christianity is experienced as an increasingly cultural and social phenomenon in the province and cities of the Roman empire, including Damascus, Edessa and the region of Antioch. While evangelization was being carried out, the distinctive formative mechanisms that could be observed for small communities of Christians were the bishops, priests, and deacons. These figures are rare but by 350 CE there could have been as many as 33 bishoprics and consequently, there may have been between 150,000 – 200,000 Christians out of a population of around 1,100,000 in Roman Syria.

In many ways, these early Christians went about their day-to-day existence with their Church community as the central point. Christians would come together for the purpose of worship and prayer and to listen to the Word of God on Sundays, on the Sunday of Orthodoxy, and other Feasts of the Saints. Baptism which has been categorized as an initiation rite was intended for the reception of the new converts regardless of their economic level. The majority of the Syrian churches also preached, chanted, performed the sacrament, and offered services for the widows, the orphans, the sick and the poor for the purpose of constructing a hospitable society that is built on faith. Church leaders writing histories about such cities as Edessa and Damascus composed sections in their history which gave historians a look at various facets of everyday life.

Women were at the forefront of the organization and active members in the early Syrian Christian Church. Most of these women were well-to-do in their respective societies, and they provided funds for the building of churches, for instance, Bassa provided for the construction of a church in Edessa. Some of them were deaconesses in charge of assistance to females in distress and assistance in baptisms. The women of the Syrian Christian Church also contributed equally with time as more and more people took up monasticism as a way of life – as ascetics, thinkers, and monastics. Thus, even though writing was performed primarily by elite women, other women of the society are illustrated to participate in all the sectors of the society.

Non-clergy laity in the same regard offered their services and financially to the Syrian churches, particularly in the urban cities. For example, only one letter – the letter 254, from two merchant brothers Aquila and Nicetes asking for prayers for safe return – in a voyage financially conducted to India is known today. These examples can be used to support the argument that the 'ordinary' Christians continue to worship as they engage in their mundane activities, thus indicating that early Christianity did not only target the elites of the society. In total, dynamic communities were formed on the basis of the integration of participation for growth.

As one of the eastern provincial territories of the Roman Empire, Syria was of great strategic value. Control of the province also gave the empire security in the eastern territories and made sure that those trade routes passing through the cities of Antioch or Damascus, leading from the Mediterranean towards Mesopotamia and the Asian regions remained safe. Syria being a strategic province for the Roman empire, every activity that threatened imperial dominance was closely monitored and this included a religious movement perceived at first as a separatist Jewish cult: Religion, and more specifically, Christianity.

Therefore, ruling throughout the first and second centuries, the Romans occasionally discriminated against emergent Christianity. The plausibility of the claim by Christians of large-scale repression has been disputed by modern historians. However, there are records of persecution of Christians by mobs including among them one of the most disgusting events that occurred in 64 CE, where Nero is said to have ordered Christians to be burnt alive for being accused of causing the Great Fire of Rome. Legal writing also registers low-level harassment and civic ordinances by Roman governors such as Aquila, Atticus, and Flaccinus who banned Christians' assemblies as gathering unlawful assembly in Syria in the late 2nd century. Yet even if its level of severity varied with time and space, the inferior status of the early Christians and their persecution pointed to the fact that many of them lived at imminent risk because of Roman domination.

This was most profoundly exhibited with the barbarian, Constantine I moving from paganism to Christianity after the battle of the Milvian bridge in 312 CE. Through Constantine's support, faith was brought to the foreground thereby reversing earlier policy. Prevailing Christianity was allowed as the official religion of the empire described by the Edict of Milan in 313CE. In the next few decades before Constantine's death in 337

CE, it metamorphoses from an outlawed cult to one of imperial patronage hence laying the foundation for its dominance over the 4th century as Rome's dominant faith. Favorable policies in regard to the construction of churches contributed to the expansion of Christianity and Christian facilities in Syria as well as its cities – previous persecution was forgotten.

The first political event that evidenced political instability in the Roman world was the death of Constantine in 337 CE because the death was followed by civil wars for leadership of the empire contrary to the stability that was evidenced before the death of Constantine. Most evidently, this shift became absolutely clear in the late 4th century at the cost of focusing on Constantinople where the Byzantine Empire emerged to rule over Rome's Hellenistically oriented eastern provinces including Roman Syria. This "Greek East" was to develop increasingly in contrast to the dissolving "Latin West" for about a millennium after the surrender of Rome to his compatriot in the sixth century.

Byzantium meant political power and ecclesiastical power, and thus a new equation of church and imperial politics in the Syrian Christian world. Other issues that dealt with the position of Chalcedon on the divinity of Christ split the opinion of the Chalcedonian church of the Byzantine Empire beginning with Constantinople with the less orthodox Syrian church that would not accept some of the decisions like one of Chalcedon's council in 451 AD. When this was combined with the ethnic hostility between Greek and Syriac Christologies, it raised the sense of the fight for dominance that is characteristic of the early Byzantine Empire, which aimed at eradicating theological diversity.

However, the late 4th and the 5th centuries A.D. are also viewed as the starting point of the monachal and ascetic movement as the major type of worship of Near Eastern Christians from Egypt to Persia. In Syria, the countryside provided the chance to pick liberty, loneliness, religious beliefs, sparse living and education. Some of the first monastics from Syria are Maron and Symeon the Stylite whose zeal in asceticism set an early preceding base when it comes to the behavioral standards of the Byzantine empire in light of Christianity. As to the experiences described by Davis, it is possible to note that there are relations between the kingdom of God and empire in its terrestrial sense.

Long before the advent of Christianity, Syria was ideally located to act as a link between the two worlds – the East and the West. But this synthesis already appears in early Syrian Christian art and the archaeological record of the immediate post-Constantinian era. For example, the use of a combination of Roman techniques such as mosaics and frescoes which blended with stylistic features associated with ancient Persia defines a particular phenomenon of the architectural combinational pattern which can be described as a combinational pattern observable in the façade of the early church. Arabic geometric floor mosaics are seen in such archeological sites as Qalb Loze and Ma'arat an-Nu'man, and room or apse decoration and being the sign of biblical conceptions and paradisiacal imagery points to Christianity and its influence over the calligraphy style originated.

In architecture, the basilica model of 4th century Rome was successfully applied to expand the church architecture for the increasing Syrian congregations supporting imperial patronage. Yet works like the elongation of a bema in the nave were done because of the regional liturgical practices borrowed from the Roman and the Syrian Christians regarding the design of sacred spaces. Cohesive holy trails existed between such places; one of them was Sergiopolis which according to history was established by Constantine. Artifacts of it and other places accentuate the interaction of Mediterranean picture language with what might be described as 'Oriental' materials like ivory and metal in the 5th and 6th centuries. What should be pointed out here is that all those accomplishments were laid early ages to develop the subsequent achievements of the Islamic era.

When early Christianity began edging out of Jerusalem sometime before the 1st century AD, Syria was one of the first regions where this ideology emerged. Other early locations of mission and theological controversy included Greco-Syrian and especially metropolitan territories like Antioch and Edessa.

The first church council is the Council of Jerusalem which is regarded as taking place around 50 AD. It is said to have met to decide whether the Gentiles should be circumcised and be subjected to the Mosaic law as was discussed in Acts chapter 15. The Syrian participants' and viewpoint dominated, which was that Gentiles do not have to be circumcised, or even follow the Jewish laws to the same extent. This made Christianity fit for growth within the Roman Empire since other factors that might have been a barrier to people accepting Christendom were done away with.

One of the first crises of the Antiochene Church occurred in 268, Paul of Samosata by rejecting the doctrine of pre-existence of Jesus. At a council of some Syrian bishops, Paul and his message were expelled and cursed, and it was determined that Jesus was fully divine as well as fully humane, and an essential practice regarding the decision-making on doctrinal issues was set here thus the local synods.

A council of the early Church that formulated one of the most well-known Christian dogmatic statements – the Niceno-Constantinopolitan Creed – was the First

Council of Nicaea, convened by the order of Emperor Constantine in Asia Minor. This creed summed up the Trinitarianism that most of the Syrian clergy professed and embraced Jesus Christ as the 'created not evolved' and being 'of the same substance' (Homoousion) as God the Father.

This Trinitarian foundation was later enhanced by the followers at the Council of Constantinople in the year 381 AD by extending the Nicene Creed to other issues for instance Macedonianism, which challenged the divinity of the Holy Spirit. Despite holding their council outside of Syria, the affirmation of the Trinity is consonant with reflections written by two Syrian theological personalities – Aphrahat and Ephrem the Syrian. It also raised the status of the bishop of Constantinople, which can be regarded as the first stage in the politicization of the main conflict between the leading patriarchates.

Finally, the age-old question of the incarnation of Christ was ascertained at the Chalcedon council in 451 AD, declaring Jesus as both fully human and fully divine in his person. However, this 'two-nature' formulation raised concern among many Syrian and Egyptian Christians because they saw that it oils over the reality of the incarnation. This split was the cause for the split of what is today known as the Chalcedonian Orthodox church and the 'non-Chalcedonian' Oriental Orthodox Church in the region.

Apart from the ecumenical councils, Syria saw many other theological experiments and controversies, which were not as famous but as important in disclosing and developing early Eastern Christian thought and the internal division. Three of these areas are the most contentious: namely, the doctrine of the Trinity, Christology and anthropology.

Syrian Christological controversies were therefore over the fact that the one and Indivisible Substance of the Father, the Son, and the Holy Spirit remained distinct personalities in order to pursue one and the same design and have the same essence. Christians refused both, Sabellianism, which eliminated the distinctions between the three persons, and strict subordinationism which placed the Son and the Spirit below the Father. This way Ephrem the Syrian managed to inspire the members of the church with his poetic work where an effort to explain the unity and yet the difference of the trinity was exercised through figures and antitheses.

More intense and longer were the patriarchal Christological debates as to how Jesus' divinity and humanity were united. This was one of the most fundamental questions that any Church in Christendom could ask, arising out of doctrines that underpinned soteriology, the academic niche that deals with the concept of salvation. Other competitor models were the Logos-flesh model of the Antiochene school and the Logos-man model of the Alexandrian school which competed for patronage of the king. It caused the Antiochene tradition to stick to maintaining two natures, as the schools of Antioch and Alexandria argued about which analogue was better to convey the hypostatic union without the mingling of the substances or the division of the person. Theodore of Mopsuestia and Nestorius are but examples of how even the best of the intellects can overstep the borderline and develop the dimorphic view of Christ's Person which, as it was deemed heretical at Ephesus (431 AD) & Chalcedon (451 AD)

The third domain committed a number of firmer questions to anthropology which include the consequences of sin, the function and powers of the human soul, the nature of things as good or bad, and the corporeal and spiritual dichotomy that is significant with worship, especially with relics, funeral rites, and icons of saints. Here the would-be reader is met with theologians of a more mystical horizon typical for the Syriac tradition like Jacob of Serugh and Philoxenos of Mabbug. As far as the anthropological topics are concerned, questions about Origen's theology and influence also feature in many of them.

It was firmly rooted by the end of the first century AD to become the antitype to Greek influence in the churches of Syria and Upper Mesopotamia. When Christians were persecuted in the Roman Empire, and were forced to shift their base eastwards, then two cities took importance, these were Edessa and Nisbis; the Doctrine of Addai, which is dated third century; and the Odes of Solomon, which are believed to be of the early part of the fourth century, were produced here. The Syriac Peshitta translation of the Bible together with the Diatessaron Gospel harmony turned theology to depend on languages and terms less-known to the Latin West.

But it was the Syrian poets, hymnographers and mystics who, in a way peculiar to the Syrians, became the forgers of theology through doxology. Some of the famous Syriac poets who also were theologians include Ephrem the Syrian and Jacob of Serugh – who wrote very many big hymns in Syriac language, containing many intertextual allusions and which created the paradoxical understanding of God which was adopted in Byzantine worship, sermons, and religious education of the Church-goers. Some other 'others' like Isaac of Nineveh, Philoxenos of Mabbug and Sahdona assimilated as Greeks did not like 'dislike of spiritual theology' with anthropological introspection that previewed motifs of later Eastern Orthodoxy.

Specific theological innovations and emphases of the Syriac tradition visible to this day include A 'Semitic' conception of the Godhead, where divine attributes and actions are depicted in terms of the body and the senses rather than philosophical; a high Mariology, concerning Mary as a model of a follower and as an instrument of sanctification; the Orthodox tradition of spiritual struggle, that is the fight of the spirit against evil; the aesthetics of the Christian experience – symbols and spaces; and poetic biblical theology as the use of concrete symbols Thus, the local genesis of Syriac Christianity and the novel cultural amalgamation that followed were an aspect of the broad storyline of Christian legacy that the subsequent streams rarely remember.

Due to its geographical position, the Syrian church was influenced by different religious currents: Greek Orthodox, Armenian, Syrian Orthodox and Arab churches were present in all the geographical parts of Syria. During the 7th century, the region fell under Muslim rule, and several heterodox currents struggled for dominance in the region; the matters of dispute being primarily concentrated in the sphere of Christology, which was in fact giving birth to new religious subjects.

First, the main Orthodox denomination in Antioch is rooted in the imperial Chalcedonian Orthodoxy linked to the Byzantine Empire, and the patriarchate of Constantinople after the council of Chalcedon held in 451 AD. In its creation, this church was Greek and was focused on large neighboring cities including Antioch, Alep and Damascus with the Greek Orthodox Patriarch of Antioch at its helm. These are fairly comparable in size but are more closely connected; the Melkite Greek Catholic Church signed the settlement of accepting the papacy in 1724 and the Syriac Orthodox Church, which is Oriental Orthodox does not follow the Chalcedonian creeds and uses the Syriac liturgical rituals.

Nevertheless, the vast majority of today's Christianity is the Arabic Neo-Aramaic speaking communities in communion with the Roman Catholic Church which was formed by the Syrian Catholic Church, that united with the universal Roman Catholic Church in 1662, and the Maronites – an ethno-religious group named after St Maron, an ascetic who evolved in Lebanon. Thus, the Nestorian Churches of the East Syrian Rite have continued to use West Syrian liturgical anaphora but with a Syriac background and embracing some Latinisms.

There are also persons who belong to other Christian denominations such as Armenian, Assyrian and Protestant in Syria; the other type of Christianity; also has its Orthodox influence and its Orientalist influence but has produced the cultivation of small, isolated communities. As it was said, conflicts and instabilities typical for the last several decades led to Christians' emigration and thus this spiritual pluralism is at risk.

The history of the Syrian church administrative organizations, clerical offices and political institutions tell the story of Middle Eastern Christians' conflicts over leadership of the church, its liturgy, finances and language as well as the struggle for power among the empires for a thousand years. Systemic relationships have lines of authority that indicate hierarchal structures.

The chief bishoprics were Antioch which communicated with what was the major east-west commercial thruway and the court of Constantine and Edessa still farther east, a site of ancient Christian hajj because of its famous letters exchanged between King

Abgar and Jesus Christ. These two important urban centres were competing for domination in the region and the Council of Ephesus in 431 determined that the position of Edessa was lower. By the church councils, the position of the Bishop of Antioch was strengthened and soon the bishop adopted the title of 'Patriarch' before 451 AD. However, rivalry continued, especially perhaps with a newcomer in the form of Constantinople.

Next to the patriarchs, there were some subordinated metropolitans controlling provinces, bishops of town and district, and priests of village churches. Genre orthodoxy, finance and legal issues were issues of contention with regard to consecration processes. The religious virtuos elaborated themselves occupying a liminal position within the state power framework as the 'faceless' decision-makers that were controlling public opinion and behavior.

The political rivalry between Constantinople and Persia caused Syriac and Greek Christianity to formally develop under one roof, that is imperial Christianity. Peculiarly, the Muslim conquests changed the structure bringing the millet system, which gave certain autonomy but kept the Jews rather limited in terms of visibility to the public. This only tended to consolidate the successiveness of ethnicity-ecclesiastical identification. Polemical issues singled out by reference to language, custom, and communal power correspond with the doctrinal disputes inherited from late antiquity. Such a complex background is the fact why the identification of various churches in Syria is rather challenging.

However, these Syriac Christians were always in the territories of empires indifferent or even hostile to their religion, but still Syrian Christianity, which arose as a local church, often developing in opposition to ecclesiastical powers, was able to create great cultural values influencing the world. Syria's obviously unique geographic position in the middle of the fertile cultural cradle that introduced it to various civilizations played a very significant role in the emergence of creative dynamism among the native Syrian scholars and artists including the Syrian Christians.

The Syriac Church's history dates back to the early church whose representatives who wrote influenced the whole world. The members of both schools Aphrahat and Ephrem the Syrian are noted for their great deeds which they contributed to poetry and hymnody. During the early period of the 3rd century, the church father by the name of Lucian of Antioch was influential in the translation of the bible and biblical hermeneutics. To this extent, in later periods reformers like Jacob Baradaeus came to lay down the spiritual dynamic of the Syrian Church as did the spiritual writers such as St. Isaac of Nineveh.

Already in the early stage of its development, the Syrian Christian scribes adopted a special type of literary language called Syriac which they translated into the Semitic vocabulary and grammar of various literatures originally written in Greek including the Scriptures and the Fathers. For this reason, as they worked tirelessly for centuries and produced a magnitude of work Syriac became the accepted language for Armenians, Persians and up to the Indian region for Christians.

The church was particularly strong in Syria and monasteries were responsible for the reintroduction of learning and scholarship; here outstanding achievements were made in theology, philosophy and the sciences. With their learning in Syriac and Arabic, they made sure that the precise part of the Greeks' legacy that was beneficial would continue to be available even in the battered fragments of the Western Roman Empire. When Islam started, the Syrian 'Christians' were the bridge between the classic civilization and the new Arab Islamic civilization.

A great contribution to world Christianity at some historical time can be attributed to the faith born out of struggle on Syrian soil. As the church of Christianity in ancient periods, the Syrian church spread its theological thought and its institutional system over Persia, India and central Asia. Thus from Syriac Christianity arose churches reaching as far afield as Arabia, Mongolia and China.

The area now known as Syria converted to Islam in the seventh century, so the heart of Christianity moved to the west. But at the same time, religious life in Syria was not alien to medieval Europe and could even contribute a little to the existing society. The first European Catholics, coming back from the Crusade or who went as pilgrims, were confronted with the cult, the construction and the decoration of Syrian Christians. These are a few of the numerous Roman church reforms which are often said to have been inspired by them.

However, in the second phase of the modern missionary movement, the Syrian Christians living abroad were also involved in evangelism among the peoples from Indonesia to the Caribbean. Fleeing the danger of exclusion, the Syrian clergy founded seminaries and disseminated revival, through which the orientations of the ancient Syrian and the Protestant traditions met.

Indeed, much of the course and character of the worldwide church is today due to invisible but formative contributions of often systematically marginalized Syrian Christians. It should therefore be noted that these communities and their living tradition are still suffering from the war going on in their countries to date, but these are voices that should still be heard in the Christian world today. In any case, the history of the Syrian Christians was a history of conflict both from within and from outside; yet the light of Christ remains steady and unbudged in Syrian territory.

The study of the history of Christianity in Syria from its origins, birth, early local followers, theological evolution, and the opportunities and threats it presents a good bird's eye view of a diverse religious heritage. Christianity was born in Syria and would not have been made by the apostle Paul the great evangelizer of the Gentiles who began the spreading of the book of the gospels out the boundaries of Jewish culture. Antioch and other major towns not only incubated the embryonic religion but were also lively contact points for many kinds of interchange between different civilizations and cultures. These communities, which were part of a wider Roman and subsequently Byzantine world, elsewhere gave rise to distinctive theological and ecclesiastical structures that still inform Christianity today.

Islam's Expansion

Muslims are no doubt one of the biggest populations of the global population, the religion started in the area that is now known as Saudi Arabia in the first quarter of the Seventh Century AD. The followers of Islam were organized into an empire one hundred years after the death of the Prophet Muhammad during which dominion in areas containing the region of Syria was established. To the early Muslims, Syria through being a province was significant to be conquered since it was almost contiguous to the central Islamic territories.

And Syria, of course, was under Roman domination before it embraced Islam – for over three hundred years Syria was the Byzantine province. The people, who comprised such parties, included Greeks, Aramaean Christians, Jews and even pagan converts. The people of this region in the pre-Islam period were exposed to a sequence of invasions by the Byzantine and Sassanian Persian empires. Due to this tiredness, it became relatively easy for the newcomers from the Muslim forces to take the region. The process of invading territories was initiated in the Arabian area after the demise of Prophet Muhammad in 632 AD. Thus by 634 CE, the Arabs were able to defeat the Byzantine Empire in the battle of Ajnadayn which ushered the Arabs into Syria. These are the last of the Yarmouk in August 636 CE that led to the surrender of Syria to the Arabs and consequently the formation of the new empire.

During the first years of Muslim domination the Arab authorities in fact did not oppose the Syrian population. All in all, the attitude of the Muslims in the religious segment was comparatively liberal and the majority of the features of the Syrian social and economic organizations did not undergo significant transformation on the advent of the Arab Muslim rulers. With time there were intermarriages and contact with the local Syrians thus improving the interaction of the Arabs. It opened the path towards Arabization and Islamization of Syria in the process of the several following centuries.

Mu'awiya governor of Syria was one of the first at the onset of the Umayyad Dynasty that was in power between 661 and 750 CE. They were able to turn it into the capital of the

Umayyads and transform it into one of the strategic points in the Caliphate's political and commercial life. In the earlier period, the Umayyads maintained the Byzantine administrative system where the new Muslims were joined by the old administrative families to govern Syria. Ancillary tax on the economy provided the initial seed money for Arab-Muslim garrison towns. As the process developed, there appeared a clearly Islamic administration that included more Muslim Arabs in the upper layers of the bureaucracy. The judiciary then incorporated the principles of Quranic justice with regard to the gradual disappearance of regional tribal laws. It is for this reason that the architectural traditions that received sponsorship from the Umayyad dynasty remain important up to this age, for instance, the Dome of the Rock in Jerusalem.

Thus, the policies of the Umayyads guaranteed Syria's incorporation into new circuits of long-distance trade in the Mediterranean and Asia and agricultural stability based on Roman irrigation. Thus free converts to Islam in Syria could discern various advantages of Muslim rule in terms of access to administering and trading. Alas, signs of this shift are already discernible even in the matter of revolution as the tendency of taxation weakened the relations between the Umayyad overclass and the overwhelmingly non-Muslim peasant population.

There were many dissident groups that rose to revolt against the Umayyads in mid 700 by the Abbasid Revolution (746–750 CE). With the aid of Persian, Arab and Syrian dissidents the Abbasids usurped the Umayade power to ascend to the throne of the Abbasid caliphate. Another sharing of the powers was the anti-

Syrian decision when the center of authorities was shifted far from the capital of Damascus. Therefore, Syria was politically unstable from the political view of other emerging political powers such as the new Abbasid Dynasty which suspected that there were still hardcore supporters of the Umayyad Dynasty in Syria. The Abbasids enhanced control in Baghdad and did not give the governors of Syria much autonomy as was the case under the Umayyads. Nevertheless, there were other small independent dynasties such as the Qarmatians and they had continued from some locations in Syria having been regarded as a constant source of concern to rulers.

The changes which the Abbasid dynasty brought into the Syrian society and its economy, influenced the region for centuries. However, even if trade for the Abbasid continued to flow through archaic circuits,

Abbasid fiscal policies imposed more of a burden on a weary farming populace. This was also true in terms of religious conversion especially because of the activities of the Sufis and because of other measures that existed to ensure that non-Muslims did not have direct access to political power. While Arabs and Muslims increasingly dominated the landed and administrative positions in the region this did not impress the non-Muslims. Religious animosity was always lurking in the background and at times gave rise to small-scale to massive-scale communal violence.

The political transformations that emerged with the onset of Islamic rule however was followed by drastic social revolution in Syrian society in the subsequent centuries of the initial Muslim conquests. The militarily defeated Christians had been slowly dying out and being replaced by Muslims and the few remaining Christians were Monophysite, Nestorian, and Melkite. Therefore, the local ethnic group of Syrians started blending with the incoming Arabia and Arabization of the area started. This was because most of the productive farmland was owned by the Muslim elite leading to a creation of religious-based socio-economic differentiation. Slavery was still there but the higher rights distinguished the 'slave gang' (mamluk) in the Muslim Syrian society.

Damascus and Aleppo became metropolitan cities and Homs was developed as well to make Syria an urbanized and multicultural society that embraced the Arab, Persian and Levantine features. The Syrian Christians and Jews contributed a lot to the economy of the country in such areas as traders, usurers, craftsmen, and suppliers of various amenities such as bakery shops and the like.

Conversion to Islam offered social advancement and the formation of fresh classes of Muslim social climbers. The ulama in mosques and madrassas over time became an intellectual elite that governed the society's ethical compass.

Economically, trade and agriculture which received the benefits of stabilities and large-scale irrigation works flourished under those subsequent dynasties of Muslims. There was manufacturing of textiles, glass, and metal products for local and export markets. Syrian products were out in circulation, and growing into covering the enlarging Islamic world and reaching Europe.

It must be noted that the successful creation of Muslim authority within the region was also the cause of the rise of Islamic institutions in

Syria. Another chronologically young grand mosque was the Umayyad Mosque in Damascus, which accommodated the new religious bureaucracies that had appeared as missionaries for the expansion of the faith. In relation to Islamic prayer, law and rituals, the duty was in the hands of religious authorities namely the imams, muftis and 'commanders of the faithful'. The Sufi mystics of Syria followed and preached the common people along with the culture of the land and this proved useful in the process of evangelism. Ash-Shafi's institution had spread its schools, legal schools in large Syrian cities. Purity and prudery rose to a different level of concern, being backed by the Quran or hadiths (proverb of Prophet Muhammad). However, Muslim rulers relied on the jizya, whereby Christians and Jews, or 'dhimmis', were protected by law and granted a high degree of autonomy in governing their own affairs, and created a diverse society with a degree of tolerance and pluralism that could not be paralleled until the present day.

Syrian societies went through some period of hostility, as well as the symbiosis of various religious denominations. Some pogroms and persecutions of the mainly Christian and Jewish 'dhimmis' took place due to natural disasters, political disorders or court scandals whenever the background of communal conflict emerged. But one also notices long years when the dhimmi communities living in Syria were incorporated into the overall Muslim framework. Some of the bourgeois layers of the native Syrian Christian and Jewish population appeared as physicians, officials, financiers and merchants, and for centuries served the Muslim rulers of the large Syrian cities. There were also relationships in the religious aspect, especially when identifying new Syriac trends of Islam, for example, Druze, Isma'ili, as well as all sorts of fraternities of Sufis, containing fragments of previous Middle Eastern spiritual practices.

The early Middle Ages in Syria saw it as a rich civilization of the Islamic empire in the 7th to 13th centuries. Before the modern period of history, Damascus, Aleppo, Homs and other large Syrian cities were notable dissemination centres of Islamic science across the entire area of the Muslim caliphate. In this period, Damascus particularly became the unrivaled centre of learning in the Muslim world through which scholars developed great breakthroughs in their different areas of study.

It can be said that Syrian scholars, Sufis, and artists imposed their imprint on Islamic culture and the Arab world at large. Medieval Syria was filled with architecture and urban planning, literature and poetry, philosophy and science, education and reading and writing. Furthermore, in connection with the translation movement, Syria can be considered as one of the leaders, which translated the classical and ancient books into Arabic. Like other Syriac institutions educational institutions, it also contributed for producing the scholars who traveled and spread the light of knowledge across between the Islamic East and the West.

After the rise of Islam in the region, Damascus was one of the earliest centres of the Islamic empire and was declared the capital of the Umayyad Caliphate in 661 CE. It became a place of convergence for the different cultures in the proceeding centuries and scholars, poets, artisans and merchants from the different parts of the Muslim world flocked to the city. Vast programs of building and public works transformed Damascus into one of the foremost cities of the Islamic Golden Age.

Craftsmen and architects, in turn, brought the novelty of stylistic transformations to the elaborated motives of stonework carving and tiling patterns. The construction of this great mosque of Damascus that was ordered in 705 CE was basically to determine a new change in the status of the city in what was gradually building up to be an Islamic civilization. Therefore, the architectural feature of a very large courtyard, and its fabulous golden dome, were followed by the layouts and domes of other mosque structures, ranging from Andalusia to central Asia. We will also note that in the Nasîbi quarter around the Great Mosque Damascene neighborhoods gradually emerged provided with baths, markets, hospitals, water supply and many intellectual conveniences.

As a center for the caliphs and wealthy patrons, it continued to be the leading city in terms of the production and accumulation of books. The refectories of the grand libraries, markets for books and paper, and paper factories of Damascus constituted some of the network of text that gave a voice to the anthology of the classical in the eastern Abbasid world. Lovers of art had long called Damascus the 'Paradise of the Orient' and, in general, there was an identification of this city with the concept of 'fine feeling' or 'sensibility'.

In the seventh and the thirteenth centuries, a company of Syrian men of letters expanded the borders of the possible in Islamic theology, philosophy and jurisprudence. Most importantly, Syrian scholars also endorsed the practice of classical erudition, which came from translations of Greek literature through Alexandria and Edessa and Persia or India.

In these polymaths, the first was Al-Farabi who was alive in 872-950 AD and was a musician. Also known as the 'Second Teacher,' after Aristotle, Al-Farabi bequeathed his brilliance to knowledge arenas such as logic, music, psychology and politics, and metaphysics to name a few. His texts were actively read from Spain to Persia, reconciling thus the traditions of the classical Greek heritage with the greatest Muslim thinkers from Ibn Sina.

Symptoms of the importance given to Islamic jurisprudence can be cited such as the Syrian jurist Ibn Abdin's book entitled Radd al-Muhtar (1783–1836). As a work of several volumes, Jassas both summarizes and elaborates on the Hanafi legal tradition which grew over centuries. It remains to be used as a reference source up to the present in Islamic courts.

During the same period, Al-Hallaj (858-922 AD) was teaching the Sufi form of Islam. He even ventured to assert that it is possible to have direct dealings with the gods. Nevertheless, his burning alive for heresy did not stop the spread of his spirituality across the Muslim world and Asia.

Favorable scholarly conditions in medieval Syrian cities promoted the development of innovational tendencies in art and literature. Later, artisans used a high level of geometric features and ornaments such as arabesques in stone carving, stuccowork and mosaic work to embellish the interior of Syrian mosques and palaces. Meanwhile, the illustrative Kufic script was being developed by calligraphers for Korans and monuments' adornment.

At this juncture, there was also a flourishing of prose as well as poetry in Syria. Al-Jahiz of Basra (c. 776 – 868 CE) worked in Damascus and he is said to be the author of more than 200 significant books of Arabic prose, humor and raconteur.

One of the fine pieces of contemplative poets whom we have is Rabia Basri (c. 714 – 801), who was born near Damascus, and later settled in Basra. She changed the face of poetry in Islam with poems of sensual love, and the final beauty of divine mutual love. Described in poetry after her death, Rabia is being considered and is still honored as the first female Sufi saint to date.

This became the golden age for cultural achievements which reflected the imprint of its culture in all parts of the Dar al-Islam and also for the dialogue with European peers during the crusades. Thus, possible motifs and ideas, scientific and literary, traveled through trade and scholars' networking. Syrian creations for as long as centuries impacted cultures like the Andalusians and the Persians.

To foster scholarship as Damascus continued to grow in prominence, the Umayyads established the city's first large-scale madrasa in 732 CE: Studied in the School of Santa Maria of the Cathedral of Damascus. Here the mayor of a provincial town transformed a Christian cathedral into an Islamic school, which teaches thirty students Islamic theology.

The situation in this respect improved under Abbasids in the late 700s CE: Damascus then had more than 50 mosques and hundreds of 'Koranic schools for children to learn by heart'. Women could also obtain education in Karrawiyyah Mosque; it is one of the oldest and popular centers in the city.

The large madrasas began in the twelfth century, especially in the big cities of Damascus and Aleppo and so marking Syria as a centre of East and West scholarship. They were the al-Halawiyya school for the Shafi legal right; the Jamaliyya Institute for medical and astronomical in addition to Islamic education. The graduates and their generations also became generations of successful clerics, jurists and scholars in various Muslim empires.

In the subsequent centuries in the times of the Ayyubid dynasty (1171-1260) and the Mamluk period (1250-1516), there were several hundred madrasas in Damascus catering to students from North Africa up to India. Wise wonder-science scholars of that era incorporated into the medical colleges of Syria and then extended it further by scholars like Ibn al-Nafis.

In the 8th century Syrian Peninsula was gradually developing into the focus of Sufism – this branch of Islamic Culture that is based on the contemplation of God through individual spiritual feeling, or passion, rather than legalistic or theological reason. In Syria, Sufi lodges referred to in Arabic as zawiya showed a number of cells for seclusion where students of Sufism may engage in meditation, and contemplation – and aiming to attain the status of Rapture.

Although works of Sufi poetry and theory emerged from various Syrian cities, the theory consisted of the pieces written by Al-Ghazzali (1058-1111 CE), Ibn Arabi (1165-1240 CE), Al-Nabulusi (1641-1731 CE).

While Sufism is considered heretical and heterodox by some scholars, it played a great role in the development of Islamic culture during this medieval age of – popularising religion and spreading across geography and people. Borrowing from the above observation, Muslims especially Sufis from Syria moved from Morocco to India for the propagation of mysticism. At the present time, there is more than ninety Sufi lodges functioning in the territory of Syria – the practices that started more than one thousand years ago and still interest people from all over the world.

Syria was under the French mandate before 1920 and till 1946 so the political as well as social setting was altered. The French authorities also sought to undermine local Islamic organizations and structures. It is over this colonial legacy that a decision has been made over the years to the Syrian Muslim identity and practice.

As soon as France captured Syria at the beginning of the League of Nations mandate, it did not take long to eliminate the decentralizing Ottoman system. Islamic local schooling systems and charity organizations, religious endowments that had sustained the communities for quite some time, were identified and dismantled. They also aimed to expunge religion from society and from the organs of government. The marginalization was considered an attack on religion by the Muslim communities in the region and scholars.

The emerging anti-colonial feeling led people to revolt against the French colonial forces for example by Sultan Al-Atrash in 1925 this succeeded in fending off the French colonial power in Damascus and other Syrian cities for some time. But these revolts were corrected with a lot of power. The repeated acts of decapitating Syrian rebels and the sustained mass incarceration of the same simply stoked the Muslims in the region.

However, nationalist movements in Syria were dominated by Islamic organizations and movements that were seen leading the independence struggle in the 1940s at the time when nationalist Syrians wanted a negotiated end to the French mandate. Another factor that brought together various Islamic interpretative communities in an anti-colonial strain was such a decision. Decolonization in the Middle East hence stimulated the immediate revival of the Islamic system in the context of Syrian society and governance.

Religious institutions in particular, have always been performing great educational and social functions in Syria based on an Islamic tradition. However, in conditions of war, economic turmoil and declining state capabilities, such non-profit networks are presented with gargantuan tasks in delivering on the above community roles.

Overall religious Syrians commonly achieve minimum levels of literacy through Quranic schools that socialize children in terms of the Quran from an early age prior to secular schooling. Damascus, the oldest operating university in Syria, Sharia Faculty which was established in 1913, is still educating Islamic jurisprudence practitioners to meet expanding needs for Islamic legal advice. During the Arab socialist era in the 1960s, religious education was replaced by state education after the schools were nationalized but later President Hafez al-Assad reintroduced the religious instructions in state schools.

Using the information about the Islamic advent and governments in Syria, cultural and scholarly activities, as well as the challenges of the modern period, a detailed understanding of Syrian Islam can be gained. The period of Islamicization of Syria through the Umayyads and Abbasids in the seventh and eighth centuries led to the formation of the social, economic and religious structures of the state that still exist nowadays. Islamic civilization's golden era was during the medieval age as cities such as Damascus became the intellectual and cultural centers for the Islamic civilization and contributed enormously to the Islamic theology, jurisprudence, philosophy and arts. Nevertheless, Syrian Muslims have also been determined and managed to maintain their culture and traditions and join interfaith cooperation and reconciliation. It is the story of expansion and progress and the story of how the Syrian Muslims contributed positively to the progress of the Muslims around the world. This rich and multi-layered interrogation of Syrian Islam contributes, however, to the understanding of other aspects of the Islamic civilization in general.

Religious Interactions

Syria region in general, has always been a place of interreligious groups and their interaction for thousands of years. Syrian religious and cultural environs of the followers of Judaism, Christianity and Islam, thus, reveal patterns of intercommunication and interchange are of significant importance for the study of the interconfessional and intercultural relations, for the processes of constructing the doctrinal and ritual traditions. It was a place where these Abrahamic faiths met and therefore has been a theatre of cooperation and theological/philosophical debates, diplomacy, exchange of goods and ideas, and sometimes wars, and civil wars.

Analyzing various aspects of the relations between religions in the ancient and medieval Syrian area offers more material to consider the factors of the interaction and conflict's enrichment.

Syria is home to Jewish history for 2900 years and Jewish people have been practising Judaism in the region. The Aramaean kingdoms that were formed in Syria also had an impact on the Jews in such a city as Damascus. Christianity started very early in the apostolic age and centered in Antioch which was one of the leading metropolitan sees. Seventh-century Islam introduced to a region, which already incorporated various religious systems, a new Abrahamic faith.

In the medieval age when the kings of the Middle East were Muslims, they didn't change their religion, Christians and Jews practiced their religion but in subject to the kings. Thus, while there were aggressive contacts, there were also many friendly and this impacted culture and religion. The gathering of knowledge and common history created rather intricate interconnection between the religions which became different in various dynasties. Analyzing the relationships of these groups it is possible to comprehend the daily life of the people in ancient Syria and the forms of organization of their communities.

The earliest known churches stemmed from the synagogues beginning in the first centuries of CE in the Syrian and Middle Eastern areas. Syria's capital now, Damascus is also famous for its part in the beginning of Christianity, when Apostle Paul converted to Christianity on its way to Damascus. For the Jews with the new faith and their traditions, one saw a range of interactions from appreciation of the common origin to accusations of treason against Judaism.

As the writings which appeared in the age of the 5th century as Doctrina Jacobi mentioned, all types of Anti-Christian rhetorics and forced conversion of Christians to Judaism. Nevertheless, tolerance linked with respecting biblical characters enabled the people to live in the region. This was due to the interference of African and European customs and beliefs after intermarriage was carried out. It is within this early period, therefore, that all positive and negative interaction between adjacent faith communities as these stabilize their self-identities and their doctrinal parameters take place.

Thus, the change of Syria into an Islamic province by 636 CE wiped out the Judaeo-Christian years from the religious background. Rashidun and Umayyad Caliphates initially extended gradually in the 7th-9th centuries and incorporated major cities like Damascus and Aleppo into the Islamic orbit. This introduced new forms of interfaith relations between the Arab Muslim elites and the more conventional pre-existing Christian, Jewish, Samaritan and other oriental local communities of the Middle East.

Some of the forms of power associated with this new state religion were new forms of bureaucracy as well. The intercommunal relations which existed during the reigns of different caliphs were not the same. The non-Muslim groups or dhimmis were given 'protected but discriminated statuses under the umbrella of Sharia law they could live their lives but had to pay taxes and abide by different laws. It thus comes as no surprise that social changes for example those that prohibited non-Muslims from owning weapons or from serving in the government changed dynamics. Conversion to Islam was more recorded after the 9th and selling centuries when it was affecting the population transforming process. Nonetheless, it is apparent that pluralistic engagement continued as change proceeded, as people in communities experienced it.

The first dynastic rule with its center in Damascus was created by the caliphate called the Umayyad Caliphate. They expanded and promoted the arts in areas such as sports, building and structure, poetry and even philosophy to mention but a few. UZBEK can be traced back to 750 CE when the Abbasid shifted to east Baghdad. Both periods can be described in terms of active and vivid interfaith relations between the representatives of different beliefs.

Also, as far as the Umayyads wanted to turn the political and juridical centres on the Islamic and Arabisation of the society, the cosmopolitan character of Damascus and greater Syria was acceptable. As the 'katib al-mamalik', the 'general director of state concerns', Sergius Bakhtishu was in office in several periods of caliph rulers. John of Damascus, the church leader wrote against the Islamic teachings, for instance, the nature of Jesus and trinity and was not persecuted. This interfaith dialogue one can anyhow trace back to Neoplatonism and Aristotelian oratory style.

For example, the Abbasids were confronted with rebellions like the one led by Thomas the Slav in 813 CE; the Abbasids' overthrow of Arab rule in Syria was only temporary. Small battles were still engaged however the large-scale wars did not hinder the achievement of assimilation of culture and knowledge. Even here it would be important to appreciate that this pluralistic cohabitation was able to support political disruptions in both the dynasties.

In the early Abbasid period and the Middle Eastern area in particular there was interpenetration and interchange between the various religions. Religious syncretism first emerged in the territory of Syria where the interpenetration of two initial religions – Christianity and Judaism with the newly introduced Islamic religion took place. The Golan contained various sites which are holy to the followers of all three Abrahamic religions including the tomb of the identificational figure of the Old Testament's Job.

Some of them later evolved new gnostic doctrines of sects such as the Druze which merged Islam with Christianity, Neoplatonism and other systems. Jim's building together with the two buildings of the grand mosque of Damascus and the cathedral of Constantine and Helen show that transitional churches are indeed hybrid constructs that include elements of the Roman, Christianity, and Islamic design. Religions also had feasting functions, sacred grounds and knowledge-based dialogues. These cultural interactions led to advances for the betterment of the two cultures.

One of them, the problem of the Trinity was one of the topics that the representatives of Christian and Muslim cultures debated in the early centuries of Islam in Syria. Discussions concerning the crucifixion of Christ and the trinity formed part of topics of discussion that went on in the courts of caliphs such as al-Ma'mun. These interactions cemented the rationalist theology, and the Kalam tradition within the Islamic society over the more strict movements. As much as the Umayyads sought to shift the political and juridical focus to Islam and the Arabisation of the society, the cosmopolitan character of Damascus and greater Syria was welcomed. Sergius Bakhtishu the 'Katib Al-Mamalik', the 'general director of state concerns', was in office in several periods of caliph rulers. John of Damascus, the church leader wrote against the Islamic teachings, for instance, the nature of Jesus and trinity and was not persecuted.

The interfaith dialogue began with Neoplatonism and Aristotelian oratory style.

For instance, the Abbasids faced rebellion such as that of Thomas the Slav in 813 CE which ousting of Arab rule in Syria was only temporary. Small-scale skirmishes were fought but the big wars did not stop the assimilation of culture and knowledge. Still, it is noteworthy that the pluralistic cohabitation sustained political disruptions in both dynasties.

In the early Abbasid period and the Middle Eastern area in particular there was interpenetration and interchange between the various religions. Religious syncretism first appeared in the territory of Syria where two initial religions that were Christian and Judaism mixed with the newly imposed

Islamic religion. Pilgrimage sites that are considered sacred in all the Abrahamic faiths including the tomb of the Old Testament figure of Job in the Golan were revered by the people of the Syrian faith.

Some of these sects at a later date developed new gnostic themes which contain some Islamic, Christian, Neoplatonic, and other features; such is the case with the Druze. In support of the statement, two buildings constructed were the classified transitional churches which comprised of the Roman, Christian and Islamic ornaments and they are the Grand Mosque of Damascus and the Cathedral of Constantine and Helen. Feast-purpose religions had feast purposes, religious grounds or holy grounds and knowledge traditions. This is remarkable, the two cultures identified engaged in cultural interactions with the purpose of increasing the two cultures.

Yet one more circle of interactions was provoked by such similar philosophic and scientific traditions originated by the Classical Greeks. Through the translations of Hunayn Ibn Ishaq and his School, it became possible to transfer a number of works in the fields of philosophy and mathematics, and especially in the field of medicine into the Arab world. Through these activities, it became possible to steer the processes aimed at overcoming the division of what was known as 'confessional states' and, at the same time, the popularization of science. Such dialogues continued during the Crusades.

Furthermore, the relations between the Christians and Muslims were multifaceted as the opposite parties could have many contacts in the Syrian land – business and friendly ones. In the early days of the Abbasid rule of Islam for example, Jewish merchants were running caravanserais from India to Europe. The Christian merchants of Armenia were privileged to have direct access to the Caliphs of Baghdad. The religious characteristic of hospitals during the Middle Ages can be seen from the example that Al-Maristan accepted sick patients irrespective of religion as Christians or Muslims in Aleppo and Damascus.

It was so during the period that could be described as relatively more liberal, especially during the Fatimid rule when Coptic Christians and Jews occupied many civil service positions. There were many petty crafts and trades which, being interlinked, subsisted through mutual federation and these included spring 'flower fairs' which resembled the Persian equivalent of the Zain day New Year festival combined with the basic Christian Easter and Jewish Passover festivals. Even though such restrictions appeared at times and even if the critics _painted_ social contact, business, art and social relations we observed that they were marked by cooperation and friendly contacts.

That is why due to the decisions of the rulers the political status and the legal rights of the religious minorities were changing all the time. The treatment given to the Christians and Jews by some Muslim governors ranged from the prohibition of Christians and Jews from practicing any trade or profession, or the imposition of heavy taxes on them, while other governors were more liberal and protected the Christians and Jews inviting them to enjoy privileges and offered them important positions in their administrations.

The Christians and the Jews were permitted to exercise a certain degree of 'separate legal personality' on certain aspects of their communal life such as marriage, divorce, and inheritance. However, the rights of Muslims could be violated and this could attract 'punishment'; a seeming contradiction. Crusaders who were Latin carried an ideal of Christian governance together with the repression of Muslims and Jews in towns conquered from them.

But in times of conflict, people also sought help from confessional communities in order to form alliances. For instance, the Byzantine emperor Heraclius mobilized Christian Arabs in Syria to battle and overthrow the Sassanian

Zoroastrians in 628 CE prior to the coming of Islam. In the same vein, the Sunni ruler Salah al-Din teamed up with Shiite Assassins and Syrian Christians, to fend off European crusaders as they encroached into their continent. This presents the dynamic and the social interchange that is engrossed by the numerous beliefs that are present in the Syrian area.

Such cultural merger led to remarkable fulfillment in different academic fields pointing out the impact of Jewish-Christian-Islamic culture in Syria in the course of the advancement of scientific philosophy, arts and so on. These cities include Damascus, Aleppo, and Antioch, and they provided the kind of network across which religious scholars felt comfortable talking to specialists in other fields, engaging in the discussion of new ideas arrivals, as well as the discussion of arriving at a fresh understanding of other disciplines. Therefore, Syria assumed the role of a multicultural scholarship center, which was translated, and studied and the manuscripts were duly preserved for future generations in Arabic, Greek, Aramaic and Hebrew.

The history of intellectual collaboration in Syria goes back to antiquity when the regions of what today is Syria became home to some of the first university cities in the Near East. Already in the 5th century B.C. schooling tradition appeared in the major Syrian cities with the help of Greeks who introduced the Syrian people to science, mathematics and philosophical thinking. In the following centuries, the traditions of the Greeks were enriched by the scholarship of Syria's local Aramic and Semitic people.

Christianity in the early centuries CE raised the level of scholarship, as churches, monasteries, priories and colleges of theology were established throughout the Levant. The monasteries were some of the centers of learning and production of knowledge, covering areas such as hermeneutics of scripture, medicine and even astronomy. Other large urban institutions were set up in the cities of Antioch and Nisibis and helped to make Syria a center of learning in the late Roman and Byzantine periods.

Another phase was the 7th-century Arab conquest of Syria which may also be considered as an important, transformative event. As old political and religious authorities emerged, Arab and Islamic rulers developed the region's cultures of scholarship as well.

Institutions of higher learning that had been around for centuries as the School of Nisibis, continued to thrive with the newfound Islamic support. However, Muslim scholars of their own tradition also founded the madrasas that emerged as crucial elements in the Islamic states' systems of schooling. Religious tolerance was the rule in ancient Syria, and these Islamic structures became a part of the universally-acclaimed learned tradition, with Jewish and Christian schools of Thought as equals.

Syrian history credited with the progress of learning in the medieval period were Jewish scholars, philosophers, and physicians. Jewish colleges in cities such as Aleppo, Tiberias, and Damascus were places where theology, law, ethics and sciences were taught in Hebrew, Arabic and Aramaic. Jewish scholars like Rabbi Moshe Hamitzri writing in

9th century Tiberias understood Arabic well enough to translate Islamic philosophy into Hebrew opening up new horizons of knowledge for Jews up and down the Levant and North Africa.

Another Jewish philosopher interested in the phenomena of Jewish philosophy was Rabbi Saadia Gaon of Fayyum, Egypt, who was active in Aleppo for several decades in the early 10th century. Saadia was one of the most popular philosophers of the Middle Ages and his works of theology, law and science were critically sensitive to both Jewish and Islamic cultures of the period. His Book of Beliefs and Opinions was aimed at explaining how principles of both Islam and Judaism should work together.

Certainly, the most recognizable Jewish academic associated with Syria was Moses Maimonides who left Andalusia to escape the Almohad dynasty and live in Galilee and Damascus in the twelfth century. Usurping an active figure as a physician, Maimonides applied in the Islamic system to establish revolutionary ideas now integral to the Judaic routine. His Mishneh Torah systematically codified Jewish law in the style of Islamic rationalist manuals and The Guide for the Perplexed combined Aristotle's philosophy and Kabbalah. Such works made Maimonides celebrated for a generation across cultures.

Syria itself was also the location in which some of the very first Christian communities emerged and thereby has a claim to achievements in the formation of theology, canon law and liturgy. Of course, there were later luminaries like Ephrem the Syrian in the fourth century who not only cultivated Syriac Christian traditions but also wrote hymns and commentaries to expand upon early Christianity, the thoughts and emotions of the religion. Another giant of the age was St John Chrysostom who, as Archbishop of Constantinople in the late fourth century spread his ideas through his preaching and writing on Christology, ethics and guidance for the Christian community.

By the fifth century, the School of Nisibis which was established near Tur Abdin became famous as a center of Syriac Christian scholarship. This was under leaders such as Narsai through whom the school provided education based on Syriac classics in addition to Jewish, Zoroastrian and Hellenistic sciences. From it, important clerical positions took shape and diffused the learned traditions of Syriac Christianity.

During the Byzantine period and the early Islamic era, Syrian Christian theologian John of Damascus wrote works such as 'The Fount of Wisdom' that characterize the Greek Orthodoxy communion – the largest communion in Christianity. It has been properly noted that his strictly Christian synthesis of faith contained much of Arabic reason and subtlety, showing that the theologian dialogued blessedly with kalam. At the same time, Syrian authors such as Patriarch Theodore Bar Koni wrote histories and commentaries targeting both Christians and Muslims with the aim of reconciliation of the two groups.

The civilization that emerged in the empire of the Muslims provided Syria with significant enhancements to its intellectual substance.

The first centers of Islamic scholarship were therefore impinged upon other traditions; for instance, Caliph al-Walid I supported the translation of Greek sciences and the School of Nisibis influenced Baghdad's House of Wisdom. Many scholars of Islamic law from Syria went on the make marvellous strides in pieces of their own.

There was the 8th century's poly-reasonable Jabir ibn Hayyan who systematized Islamic alchemy in some works that European alchemists used for centuries. Another great scholar was Thabit ibn Qurra, a 9th-century scholar who lived in Harran and who composed over two hundred books on mathematics, astronomy, logic and natural philosophy amongst other subjects. Similarly in Harran, the Brethren of Purity wrote the Encyclopedia of the Brethren of Purity – an immense work on theology, metaphysics and natural philosophy that had influenced Jewish, Greek and Persian literature.

Others further extended these horizons in the later centuries. The 13th-century Damascus-based Averroes introduced revolutionary rationalized philosophies to the Islamic Aristotle and the Latin West where he was translated by such personalities as Michael Scot. At the same time, people like Ibn al-Nafis used logic and medicine to lay the foundations for an understanding of pulmonary circulation long before European anatomists. Such giants proved that the general practice of different sorts of elitist trends in Syria had led to inventions in every epoch.

There are examples of true theological brotherhood between the two faiths that can easily be traced in the history of Syria. During the ninth century in Tiberias, two people composed mystical tracts interpreting Aristotle: the Jewish master Moshe Hamitzri and the Islamic savant Abdullah Ibn Saul. Samuel of Nehardea on the 10th century Aleppine institution of the House of Wisdom included think tanks where masters of the Torah, the New Testament, and the Quran synchronized and exchanged views and interpretations of the scripture among scholars, Jewish, Christian, and Muslim. Yet one could observe that the religious barriers did not exist in their age, for example, Rabbi Hanokh's son Rabbi Hasdai ibn Shaprut – the statesman and physician to the Muslim caliph.

Another famous case is the dialogue of the Arab philosopher Ibn Rushd (Averroes) of the 12th century in Damascus who had an exchange with his Jewish colleague Rabbi

Joseph ibn Shoshan. For their discourses on divine law were rather free and inspired one another — while Ibn Rushd's works carried Aristotelian logic to Europe, Ibn Shoshan used Islamic rationalism in his rabbinical decisions. Scripture concordances and alumur saw works of the collaborative contemplative guilds far into the Mamluk.

That is why interfaith partnerships produced unique cultural crops. Experts enriched each other's fields in rather genuine discussions, attaining new combinations that advanced human wisdom. Altogether, the generation enabled the passing through of sources belonging to distinct languages and religions to share the pearls of antiquity with the new generations. Finally, their devotion to reason over religious beliefs encapsulated the spirit of some of the best-known centres of learning in the medieval world such as Damascus in the twelfth century.

It may be understandable that religious scholars presented indispensable activities for the transmission and preservation of knowledge across cultural divides in Syria. Indeed, monastic scriptoria, as well as libraries of madrasa and scholars, collected priceless stocks of Greek, Syriac, Persian and Arabic writings. Most of this patrimony would have been simply lost and translating it had the effect of archiving texts into new media of language.

Christian, Jewish and Muslim translators offered translations into the partner languages which were word-by-word editions that made the exchange between the various religious intellectual environments possible. For instance, the Christian translator of the 7th century Sergius of Reshaina translated basic texts on medicine by Hippocrates and Galen into Syriac. Drawing from original sources.

These exchanges were further important for sciences that built on the Greek substratum ranging from geometry to astronomy. In this way, Syrian scholars avoiding the approach of the loss of knowledge saved and promoted Antiquity's achievements beyond the Mediterranean comprehensive. Thanks to their thorough commitment to preservation, these works can be mentioned among the greatest philosophical actions in world history.

Syrian art also experienced cross-cultural contacts, which, in the sphere of visual arts, were perhaps most intense. The Umayyad dynasty that emerged in Syria in the 7th century was followed by an age of religious artistic interaction of significant compatibility. The mosques in Damascus and Ramla also adopted such features borrowed from Syria's Byzantine Church such as mosaic artwork and cruciform laid-out plans with hypostyle hall additions.

Subsequent Mamluk cities showed expressiveness as the Madrasas assumed the architectural forms of church basilicas. This was articulated through interiors where calligraphy of Islamic inscription combined with fresco, a technique that was used in the 13th century, Aleppo's Mansouri Great Madrasa. In miniature illustration, with Christian and Muslim artists side by side, were left brilliant works such as the David Chronicles of the thirteenth century commissioned by Aleppo's Christian nobility. Lay history points to the transference of stained-glass techniques from Christian ateliers to of mosque designers as early as the 14th century.

These two currents intermingled seamlessly to a point that during what could be argued as the pinnacle of Islamic rule in Syria, scholars were unsure how to pinpoint what they considered as 'Muslim art'. Sculptural and architectural masterpieces emerged to be screens on which Judaism, Christianity and Islam pooled into a common medieval aesthetic. Their amalgamation is the perfect justification for the multiculturalism that Syrians have always been proud of.

While in Syria scholars not only made efforts to keep the legacy of schemes from the previous eras but also started exploring new horizons that triggered the rest of the world to move forward in science. Practical Innovations of engineers in the 9th century Umayyad period were as follows, From norias, deplored water to flush toilets. At the same time, the optics experiments that Ibn al-Haytham made in the city of Basra in the eleventh century allowed us to determine the scientific method several hundred years before Europe. His Book of Optics dispelled Greek intromission theories through hypothesis and reason on optics, vision perception psychology for modern science.

As was the case with translation, the interfaith relationships itself bore the seeds of these philosophies. Saadia Gaon and Al-Kindi, Jewish and Muslim scholars, respectively, under the influence of Aristotelian logic-imposed rationality between faith and reason. Their works contributed to the formation of the concept of science as the source of knowledge precious together with the Biblical one. Subsequently, Moor, 12th-century writer Ibn Bajah built on Neoplatonism in Andalusian and Syria and contributed atoms, void space and rudimentary atomic theory 400 years before they did in Europe. While compilers such as Gerard of Cremona introduced Averroes' metaphysical and philosophical writings to widen the sphere of scholastic concern throughout Europe.

Syrian multiculturalism therefore endowed its diverse heirs with vision and technology to forge revolutionary interpretations in vision, healing, star-gazing and even the concept of reasoning. Had there been no free and wide-spreading debate across the religious divide then, perhaps scientific advancement could well have been stalled or possibly diverted for the later generations.

The cultural exchange also bestowed upon Syria a common literary heritage that is today still being commemorated. More than the Divine Comedy or the Shahnameh, these epics emerged from the interactions between the Abrahamic faiths of Syria's Middle Ages. There are such specialists like Ephrem the Syrian who wrote hymns where it is possible to distinguish features of SyriacMetrics poetry as well as Jewish and Zoroastrian elements. Afterward, there was an Islamic writer known as Al-Ma'arri, who developed Arabic verses by imitating Ephrem and the Greek meters. Meanwhile, Buhturisht, a Christian man of letters of the 9th century in Baghdad, introduced the Arabic poetry's qasida form into Syriac literature.

Important collections, too, were created in interfaith salons. Incorporated in the Encyclopedia of the 10th Century Brethren of Purity are didactic fables and verses that converse traditional Jewish Midrashic, Christian and pre-Islamic Arabic. Four hundred years later, books from the 12th century such as Damascus Chronicles told of histories merging stories from Judaea, Orthodox Christian and Islamic traditions in exquisite koa-veneered books.

Epics that span religious divides are equally informed by Syrian craftsmanship as are repetitive ones. While writing the Shahnameh, Ferdowsi used the Syrian Christian Epic of Ephraem translated and Jewish Apocrypha brought to him by Christian and Jewish scholars in Baghdad. Syrian musicians took with them, into Andalusian zajals and their European variances, the art forms such as maqam modal theory. Not a single cultural field escaped disruption by the Syrians' talent for assimilating countless forms of storytelling.

Education led the great cities such as Damascus, Aleppo and Antioch, the institutions where scholars' meetings were productive. The School of Nisibis demonstrated how founded under Christian patronage, centers first flourished for centuries as safe havens of diverse currents. It seems that even after the Islamic conquests the school continued to transmit sciences in Syriac to Muslim as well as native Assyrian students up to the ninth century.

The pluralistic aspect continued to be captured in institutions that were established under Islam by being founded anew. Intellectually, al-Qarawiyyin University of Fes dates back to the 8th century Umayyad period when scholars from Syria put in place Quranic and grammar curricula that are still standard in defining education in the Islamic world. More than half a millennium later in another Mamluk city of Damascus, religious diversity was actively promoted when founding institutions such as the Mansouriya Madrasa, in which debates were held for theology for Christianity and Judaism as well as for twelve branches of Islamic law.

The academies fostered such epistemic communities where scholars could link each other across considerable distances. Syria's heritages were relocated by means of travels for education and intellectual pursuits by individual thinkers such as Maimonides in Cairo, Ibn Sina in Hamadan, and Michael Scot at the University of Oxford. Such productive transmissions substantiate that not simply

Syria's geographical position affected the world's crossroads, but also the progress of knowledge. Their exchanges and scholarship left behind a daring precedent that is both reasonable and pluralist.

Preserving Religious Heritage

Syria has various religious heritage sites that come with cultural and architectural significance depicting Syria's various religious affiliations. These are the religious buildings that have acted as the cradle of Syrian spiritual and cultural beliefs starting from mosques, churches, synagogues, temples and other types of shrines. These sites are not only the buildings but contain the history and culture and beliefs and traditions and art of different spiritual groups of this world.

In fact, the importance of religious sites does not only lay in the sacramentary qualities that they offer. It has been found to be vital, particularly in the area of the management of the cultures of the nation. They are physical evidence of the existence of this faith and help in understanding the changes in religious occurrences, the relations between the religions and the overall history of Syria. They are also significant for tourism centres, schools and for the Syrians' togetherness creating a spirit of belongingness and pride.

The importance of the preservation of religious heritage sites in Syria can be summed up for several reasons. First of all, it provides for historical continuity. They are like monuments that give their occupants a rich record of the country's history and by ensuring their conservation we can always see the extremely consistent link between the past and the present. Second, the preservation of cultural tourist sites enhances on diversity of cultures. Syria possesses many cultural and religious diversities and historical monuments which include the following; To maintain such sites serves to mark and to foster the appreciation of multiculturalism.

Religious diversity in Syria is always rather vast and each of the communities has its history and background. Some of the major religions are Islam, Christianity and Judaism but there are also minorities of Druze, Alawites and Yazidis among others. This diversity in religious practices has influenced the cultural development of Syria and in turn the country boasts of several historic religious buildings and artworks.

There some attempts have been seen that religious communities have put efforts to protect their heritage sites. Popular initiatives often encompass inter-faith cooperation: it implies that even with the existing differences in beliefs, people can always stand united. For example, the Christian and Muslim parties built churches and mosques. In the Christian-dominated city of Maaloula, those people have united to restore the church of St ·Thecla which has been impacted by the war.

In Aleppo, both Muslims and Christians have worked together on the rehabilitation of such sites as the Great Mosque of Aleppo and the Church of the Holy Forty Martyrs Armenian Apostolic Church. These cooperative processes do assist in managing the conservation and protection of the buildings but also assist in the relationships between the specifically different believers of the different religions.

There are always considerations of culture in practices of preservation as this is a sensitive area. Many sites in Syria that could be of great importance are religious centers for certain groups of people, and any preservation initiatives must take those people into account.

This is also a case of incorporating all the various religious groups who were a part of Syria's history and can therefore be part of the preservation projects. This can be puzzling in a country that has had a very sensitive religious scene and one that is still a subject of debate, but it is a necessary part of building a sense of stewardship of the heritage of the Syrians.

Among the most remarkable features of the architectural development in Syria, is the phenomenon of syncretism based on the prosperity of cultural and religious construction. A good number of historical structures in Syria are the result of an interconnection of multiple art styles and motifs, which have been borrowed from other cultures and religions.

For example, the Umayyad Mosque in Damascus is a clear example of this syncretism. The structure of origin was built as the temple for the Roman gods but was later used as the Christian Basilica as well as a mosque. This is evident in the architectural structure of the mosque where one gets to find such things as the Roman columns, Byzantine mosaics and the Islamic calligraphic inscriptions which interconnect here.

Another of the essential aspects of the religious history of the Syrian state is artistic representations of faith. These extraordinary intercessory arts and crafts – from Islamic calligraphy and geometric designs on the walls to frescoes and Christian icons – are not mere ornamentation; they convey religious sentiments. These are depicters of religious cultures and may be used in understanding the religious practices of different religious groups.

In the city of Aleppo itself, there are some masterpieces of carving and mosaics, which demonstrate the tendency of the different epochs and cultural circles. This church is the Church of Saint Simeon Stylites which contains frescoes that tell pictorial stories of the life of Saint Simeon and the early Christians.

Religious sites in Syria also are a clear manifestation of the cultural interaction and, again, bearing the impression of centuries. This has placed the country in a strategic position as a center of exchanges in terms of ideas, goods as well as art. This cultural interaction is especially seen in the artistic developments and techniques that are reflected in the religious art architecture in Syria.

For instance, the Great Mosque of Aleppo has Seljuk, Mamluk, and Ottoman structures detailing the different times of the Muslims' dominion in the area. Damascus and Aleppo are home to one of the oldest synagogues known as the Jobar Synagogue which boasts of Jewish Islamic and even Christian artwork.

Education and awareness will have a key role to play in the future. This is important because doing so gives exposure to the said areas and the need to protect them which may be useful in the promotion of the campaign for the protection of the historical sites. Education can also help in the improvement of cultural sensibility and therefore religious intolerance and respect for other people's beliefs.

Thus, it is possible to name several ways concerning the promotion of public awareness of the religious past of Syria including the school programs. Another thing that is also essential to mention is that not only museums, exhibitions, and other cultural events can also play the role of problem awareness.

Therefore, such public participation is going to be crucial in maintaining religious heritage in Syria. The protection of such places is not just about the question of technicalities and costs; it is one social-cultural practice in the preservation of history. For this reason, negotiation with communities is helpful in that it will ensure that those in the vicinity of the particular sites have a similar appreciation of the value of the particular sites.

It can be at the awareness, the planning, and the implementation level, but also in the functional sense of the word, conservation of resources. It can also include the process of placing efforts in front of the orientation of the facilities for the support of the programs for cultural tourism and for the sustaining of economic revival, which in turn makes the milieu for a better future for these landmarks and all the people dwelling in them.

It is thus essential to preserve this religious asset as much as it is complicated to do it in Syria in particular. I have seen these sites as not only physical structures of buildings and facilities, but histories, arts, and cultural and social recall. They are designed to depict beliefs, ceremonies and customs of the various religious communities existing in the territory of Syria and, therefore, they are various.

Disclaimer

Everything shared in this book should be considered as educational and informative in nature. The author and publisher shall not be responsible for any loss or damage suffered by any reader directly or indirectly through reading of, reliance on, and use of information that only the author and the publisher know at the time of writing this book.

Some of the suggestions given and the approaches recommended in the book may not be applicable to certain circumstances. The author and the publisher shall not be held responsible for any damages caused as a direct result of the use or non-use of the information presented in this book.

It is understood that readers should not rely on it for professional solicitations such as medical, legal, financial, and other related opinions. If any professional help is needed, then advice of a competent professional person should be taken.

The author and the publisher will not be held responsible for direct, indirect, special, or consequential damages or any other costs whatsoever arising from the use of the information present herein in this book.

About the Author

Maher Asaad Baker (In Arabic: ماهر أسعد بكر), is a Syrian musician, author, journalist, VFX & graphic artist, and director. He was born in Damascus in 1977. He grew up with a dream of being one of the most well-known artists in the world, and he has been working hard to achieve it ever since.

He started his career in 1997 when he was only 20 years old. He had a passion for technology and media, and he taught himself how to develop applications and websites. He also explored various types of media-creating paths, such as music production, graphic design, video editing, animation, and filmmaking. He was not satisfied with just being a consumer of media; he wanted to be a creator of media.

Reading was another source of inspiration for him. He was always surrounded by books as a child, thanks to his father's extensive library. He read books from different genres, topics, and perspectives. He read books for knowledge, for wisdom, for entertainment, for enlightenment. Reading stimulated his imagination and curiosity. Reading also developed his writing skills.

He did not start writing professionally until later in his life, as he was busy with other projects and pursuits. But when he did start writing, he proved himself to be a talented and prolific writer. He wrote articles for various newspapers and magazines on topics such as politics, culture, society, art, technology, and more. He wrote books that were informative and insightful. He wrote books that were creative and captivating. He wrote books that were best-selling and award-winning.

He is most known for his book "How I wrote a million Wikipedia articles", where he shares his experience of being one of the most prolific contributors to the online encyclopedia. He reveals his methods, techniques, strategies, and secrets of writing high-quality articles on any subject in record time. He also discusses the benefits and challenges of being a Wikipedia editor in the age of information overload.

He is also known for his novel "Becoming the man", where he tells the story of a young man who goes through a series of transformations in his life. The novel explores themes such as identity, masculinity, self-discovery, love, loss, and redemption. The novel is based on his journey to becoming who he is today.

Copyright © 2024 Maher Asaad Baker